Arnold

Play

Annie Wobbler, Four Portraits – of Mothers, Yardsale, Whatever Happened to Betty Lemon?, The Mistress, Letter to a Daughter

Yardsale and *Whatever Happened to Betty Lemon?*: 'From his earliest plays, Wesker has always delineated women with understanding and sympathy. Both these qualities are present here . . . each character convinces one equally of the depth of her suffering and of the resilience of her spirit.' *Sunday Telegraph*

The Mistress: 'Women as victims . . . traditional Wesker themes . . . wrapped up marvellously here and re-presented . . . a fascinating evening in the theatre.' *Kaleidoscope*, BBC Radio 4

Letter to a Daughter: 'Wesker breaks new ground . . . a moving depiction of a doubt-ridden single mother . . . a finely crafted piece of theatre.' *Jewish Chronicle*
'A very female piece, moving at times, funny at times, but most often radiant with an extraordinary energy and dramatic tension.' *The Stage*

Annie Wobbler: 'The interesting common denominator is this spirit of self-examination, and a marvellous technical feat of writing.' *Financial Times*
'Arnold Wesker is a gifted dramatist . . . *Annie Wobbler* is fascinating . . . a rare evening.' *Birmingham Post*
'The kind of opportunity any actress would relish . . . sharply defined.' *Evening Standard*

Four Portraits – of Mothers with *Yardsale* won the £10,000 Georges Bresson prize.

Arnold Wesker was born in Stepney in 1932. His education came mainly from reading books and listening to BBC radio. He pursued many trades, from furniture maker to pastry cook, until 1958 when *Chicken Soup with Barley* was read by George Devine and produced at the Belgrade Theatre, Coventry. *Roots* followed in 1959, and together with *I'm Talking About Jerusalem* the three plays created an enormous impact as the 'Wesker Trilogy' at the Royal Court in 1960. His other plays include *The Kitchen* (1961), *Chips with Everything* (1962, voted 'Play of the Year'), *Their Very Own and Golden City* (1965; winner of the Italian Premio Marzotto Drama Award in 1964), *The Four Seasons* (1965), *The Friends* (1970), *The Old Ones* (1972), *The Wedding Feast* (1974), *Shylock* (1976), *Love Letters on Blue Paper* (1977), *Caritas* (1981), his six one-woman plays (1982–92), *One More Ride on the Merry-Go-Round* (1985), *Lady Othello* (1987), *When God Wanted a Son* (1997), *Break, My Heart* (1997) and *Denial* (2000). Arnold Wesker has also written for film and television and published several collections of poems, short stories, essays and lectures.

by the same author

ARNOLD WESKER

Plays: 2
One-Woman Plays

Annie Wobbler
Four Portraits – of Mothers
Yardsale
Whatever Happened to Betty Lemon?
The Mistress
Letter to a Daughter

introduced by the author

Methuen

METHUEN CONTEMPORARY DRAMATISTS

3 5 7 9 10 8 6 4 2

This edition first published in the United Kingdom in 2001 by
Methuen Publishing Limited
11–12 Buckingham Gate, London SW1E 6LB

Annie Wobbler was first published in Italian in the programme of Teatro
Festival Parma April 1986
First published in English in *Words International* December 1987 and
January 1988
Copyright © 1986, 1987, 1988 by Arnold Wesker

Four Portraits – of Mothers first published in *Stand* Winter 1987–8
Copyright © 1987 by Arnold Wesker

Yardsale first published in *Plays International* April 1987
Copyright © 1987 by Arnold Wesker

Whatever Happened to Betty Lemon? first published in German in
Englisch-Amerkanische Studien,
Munich 1986
First published in English in *Plays International* April 1987
Copyright © 1986, 1987 by Arnold Wesker

The Mistress first published by Penguin Books 1989
Copyright © 1989 by Arnold Wesker

Letter to a Daughter first published by Penguin Books 1994
Copyright © 1994 by Arnold Wesker

Collection and introduction copyright © 2001 by Arnold Wesker

The right of the author to be identified as the author of these works has
been asserted by him in accordance with the Copyright, Designs and
Patents Act, 1988

Methuen Publishing Limited Reg. No. 3543167

A CIP catalogue record for this book is available from the British Library

ISBN 10: 0 413 75840 0
ISBN 13: 978 0 413 75840 8

Typeset by Deltatype Ltd, Birkenhead
Printed and bound in Great Britain by
Cox & Wyman Ltd, Reading, Berks

Caution

Contents

Chronology of first performances

Sullied Hand (Edinburgh Festival)   1984
Yardsale (Edinburgh Festival; Lyric Theatre
   Studio, 1987)   1985
One More Ride on the Merry-Go-Round
   (Phoenix, Leicester)   1985
Bluey (BBC Radio 3)   1985
Whatever Happened to Betty Lemon?
   (Théâtre du Rond-Point, Paris; Lyric
   Theatre Studio, 1987)   1986
Beorhtel's Hill (Towngate Theatre, Basildon)   1989
The Mistress (Festival of One-Act Plays,
   Arezzo; Sherman, Cardiff, 1997)   1991
Letter to a Daughter (Sanwoolim Theatre
   Company, Seoul; Edinburgh Festival, 1998)   1992
Three Women Talking (Northlight, Chicago)   1992
Wild Spring (Bungaku-za, Tokyo)   1994
Blood Libel (Norwich Playhouse)   1996
When God Wanted a Son (New End Theatre)   1997
Break, My Heart (Sherman Theatre, Cardiff,
   and HTV)   1997
Barabbas (BBC TV)   2000
Denial (Bristol Old Vic)   2000

For more information about the author please visit
website www.arnoldwesker.com

Introduction

These plays for one actress were written over a period of ten years – 1982–1992. Tucked between were written six full-length plays for casts of between three and one hundred and fifty, a 90-minute radio play for seventeen characters, a libretto for an opera of my play *Caritas*, two one-act plays for schools with casts of seven plus, two TV adaptations and a film based on novels by Arthur Koestler, Doris Lessing and George Orwell.

I feel the need to establish such a context because some might imagine one-woman plays were *all* I had written in those ten years. Not that I am apologising for writing this cycle for one actress. There is a view that dismisses the one-person play as of little consequence because they are 'for one actor only'. Why? We do not dismiss the great works for solo instrument simply because they are 'for one instrument only'. Is it an inconsequential part of his talent that has gone into the composition of the magnificent Beethoven sonatas for piano – the 'Moonlight', the 'Pathétique', the 'Appassionata'? I do not presume to compare myself with Beethoven but the principle is the same – the best of whatever is my talent and intelligence has gone into these plays, which in no way do I consider slight pieces.

And I persist in describing them as plays rather than monologues. A monologue is one person speaking but not *engaged in any action*; it suggests a character thinking out loud and addressing no one else. A *play* for one actor on the other hand suggests a character responding to a situation, involved in an action, engaged in an exchange of some tension.

With those definitions in mind none of these plays can be described as monologues. In each there is either 'someone else' being addressed – whether it is Annie Wobbler talking to 'madam and God' offstage, or Annabella talking to imaginary journalists, or Betty Lemon talking to her noose. And there is activity: Stephanie cooking or making trips to overcome her depression; Samantha cutting out the pattern for one of her dresses; Betty Lemon grinding coffee. Frequently both are happening – someone is being addressed while an action is taking place: Ruth talking to her daughter while packing her suitcase; Deborah shopping into her supermarket trolley while talking to another shopper.

And they contain most of the ingredients one expects to find in a play: complex structure, cause and effect, development, rhythm, dramatic dialogue, metaphor, resonance and interaction between people – even if only different people within the one person. They may not be plays that succeed in what they set out to achieve – public and posterity will judge that. I write simply to ask that they be considered for what they are, not dismissed for what they are not.

★　★　★

When writing about our writing we're involved in the process of trying to understand what we've written.

There are two vistas to be contemplated when writing a play, perhaps in the creation of any work of art: the vista ahead, from the starting point of the blank page to that end towards which we struggle, sometimes confidently, sometimes tentatively – it could be called 'the vista of what one is doing'; and the vista from the end looking back – which must then be described as 'the vista of what one has done'. And intention may not necessarily correspond with the result.

Let me employ another image: the tree (imagine it is very fast growing). We plant what we know will be an elm (as we most of us know what we want our play to be about when we begin); and sure enough there it comes, forming tall with clusters of small flowers budding before the appearance of its serrated leaves, as we had imagined. What we didn't imagine, what we could not control were the branches: where they were positioned, how they shaped. Some thrust out misshapenly, others had a strength and beauty we couldn't predict, some grew too closely together or spread longer than we thought necessary for the right balance. If we weren't careful there would be too many dark areas, or the tree would topple. So we cut and prune and make it as near as possible correspond to what we had intended in the first place.

It can never be precisely the same, however. 'The vista of what one was doing' produced an elm, that's for sure, but those branches – we knew there would have to be branches, we *wanted* branches, but those unpredictable shapes – *they* are the 'vista of what one has done'. I'll be specific.

Annie Wobbler. A play in three parts, each part the portrait of a different woman. I had begun wanting to recreate a woman who had been a childhood memory and whose name really was Annie Wobbler. I gave up after a few pages, unable to continue for many months until I'd written a play called *Caritas* – about a fourteenth-century anchoress – and had wanted the actress, Nichola McAuliffe to perform the role in the National Theatre's production. She had recently made an impression on me and the director, Peter Farago, who'd directed her in *The Wedding Feast* at Birmingham Rep. The National's casting director thought her not good enough. I'd prove them wrong, I vowed, which gave me the impetus to return to *Annie Wobbler* and write it for Nichola. When I had finished the first portrait of the old bag lady I dried. What would the second one be about? And why on earth was I writing a play for an unknown actress with protruding teeth and a nose that seemed to have grown straight out of her forehead? I should be writing plays for stars. What *was* there about her?

I can't remember if I asked myself 'what *was* there about her?' or 'what *is* there about her?' I know only that the moment I asked the question I had the first line of the second portrait, Anna, a gawky student who's making-up for her first date having just earned her BA (Hons) in French. She's in black underwear regarding herself in the mirror and asking her reflection 'what *is* there about you?'

When finished I was again stumped. What could I possibly write for the third portrait? I cruised through my notes, those legendary scraps most writers throw into a box file or drawer and rummage through in bleak times; and there, on the back of a card or a small envelope were the words uttered by the American novelist, Judy Rossner, who had recently enjoyed a phenomenal success with her – I think fourth – novel *Waiting for Mr Goodbar*. I had asked her, at a small dinner given by our mutual publisher, Tom Maschler, what did it feel like to be suddenly rich and famous. I can't recall precisely the words of her reply that I recorded on that scrap of paper (something like 'fucking Empress of China'); whatever they were it gave me the idea for the third portrait: a writer rehearsing three different interviews in which she plans to present three different personas – the modest writer, the arrogant writer, and the real writer crippled by doubt and self-denigration.

What I have described is 'the vista looking ahead'. I had wanted to recreate a childhood memory, a defiant young woman who cared about her sexuality as well as her brains, and a writer who, like myself, stumbled between arrogance, modesty and searing self-doubt. I think I succeeded in that. But looking back over the years I realise I've written about women driven by a profound sense of disharmony within themselves, or of something missing.

Sarah Kahn in *Chicken Soup with Barley*:
A man *can* be beautiful. I hate ugly people – I can't bear meanness and fighting and jealousy – I've got to have light . . .

Beatrice in *The Four Seasons*:
I can't bear little men: mean, apologetic, timid men, men who mock themselves and sneer at others . . . Peace, majesty and great courage – never. I've found none of these things . . .

Connie in *When God Wanted a Son*:
Look at my face. The skin is hardening. I see lines. I feel lumps. I see blotches. I feel terror . . . Hold me, comfort me. It goes. I feel it going. No anchor, me. No anchor. Anchor me, Mother . . .

Christine in *Caritas*:
I see the world's shape. God shows me the world's shape. I see its joins, I see its links, I see what clasps and holds it together. There's the hole and there's the dowel, there's the dovetail, mortise, tenon. Oh! Oh! I hear the flower blossom, see the harvest grow. I know the colour of the wind, the dark in light. Oh! Oh! It joins and locks and fits and rhymes . . .

Maeve in *Break, My Heart*:
Michael, will you let me look for a job? You've got yours. Very satisfying it must be – joinery. Making things fit. Wish I could make things fit. There's not

much round here, I know, but something . . . Bring in a few more bob, get me out of the house.

Finally the three Annies in *Annie Wobbler*.

Annie:

Most of the day I'm dead. I'm dead or not there. Don't know where I go because when I come back I can't think where I've been . . . Got all the parts wrong when they put me together. Needed to rub me out and draw me again.

Anna:

What is there about you? That trunk surely doesn't belong to those legs. I think I'd better go back to the shop and get them to sort this lot out, there's been a terrible mix-up here somewhere.

Annabella:

I keep getting this urge, you see, to write poetry, it's a very strong urge and I become filled with a special kind of – kind of – how can it be described? An incorporeal expectation. A bit like being on heat. And out it comes, this poetry, this selection of words and images I *think* is poetry. And it's shit. And a pain. Such a pain. You've no idea the pain it is to begin with this heat, this fever, this sense that an astonishing assembly is about to take place and all that assembles is shit . . .

I could quote more. The point is made.

An aside: I have never read a review that has observed such a branch stemming from the main trunk of my works, or known of any PhD student identifying it as a theme to be explored for their thesis. Academics claim to see in a writer's work what the writer cannot see. Very few do. 'Angry Young Man' continues to be the limited prism through which my generation is meaninglessly viewed. The women in my work are rarely identified or explored for their significance.

I don't know why these women stride through the plays and stories. Was it because I had a strong mother whom I loved and admired and for whom I felt a deep sadness that she lived a wasted life? Or is it because, as some say, most male artists have a stronger feminine nature than other men? I don't know if that's true – I'm not aware of the evidence. Or is it because given the choice of the company of men or women I would – finding most men predictable and pedantic – choose the latter? Perhaps it's a combination of all three: strong mother, feminine nature, and a disposition to find women more interesting, more vivacious. I'm not sure, I really am not. I can only look back at 'the vista of what one has done' and observe the many women there; and whether they are there as mother, as wife, as mistress, as devourer, survivor, victim, daughter, whether defiant, supportive, frustrated, mean, suffering, or joyous, they all seem driven by this sense of disharmony, of something missing.

It seems to have been so ever since Eve thought there was something more to life than Paradise. And then of course when Paradise was lost it became Paradise that was missing from life and for which she searched.

Arnold Wesker
Blaendigeddi
July 2000

Annie Wobbler

A play in three parts

Annie Wobbler *was originally written for the talents of my friend Nichola McAuliffe.*

Annie Wobbler was first broadcast in German by Suddeutscher Rundfunk on 3 February 1983, under the title *Annie, Anna, Annabella*. The English-language premiere took place on 5 July 1983 at the Birmingham Repertory Theatre Studio, with Nichola McAuliffe, directed by the author and designed by Pamela Howard. This production subsequently transferred to the New End Theatre, London, on 26 July 1983 and was revived on 13 November 1984 at the Fortune Theatre, London. The New York opening was on 16 October 1986 at the Westbeth Theater Center with Sloane Bosniak, directed by Gerald Chapman.

Annie Wobbler was conceived to be performed without an interval. During the run in Birmingham I became anxious about the audience's ability to concentrate for 85 minutes non-stop, so I asked Nichola to give one performance with an interval. She was reluctant but agreed. She hated the break. I questioned members of the audience. All said they didn't want or need an interval. It broke their concentration. I believe greater impact is achieved, and of course the actress is challenged to present a *tour de force*, if there is no break and the action is continuous. I have laid out the text here (pp. 24–5) to show how it must be done if an interval is insisted upon.

I have indicated Cockney dialect only here and there by dropping odd 'h's. It would have made tiresome reading carried throughout. But a Cockney is certainly what Annie is.

ACT ONE

PART ONE

Annie Wobbler

Music: 'Ah, Sweet Mystery of Life'. *

Part of a two-roomed tenement attic flat. Stone steps lead up to the landing outside. The landing serves as the kitchen in which there is a gas stove and an old wire-meshed kitchen-cabinet with a drop-leaf serving as a table. Alongside is a deal wooden stool. At the foot of the steps, in a corner, is a sink with only a cold water tap.

ANNIE WOBBLER, *part-time tramp, part-time cleaning woman, is in the last stages of scrubbing the 'kitchen'. She must once have been a maid in an upper-class household, her speech and manner carry the echoes of 'refainment' – years of decline have made her eccentric. Everything she wears is black with odd touches of green – voluminous skirts hide all manner of things. The hat on her head seems ever to have been there.*

ANNIE *speaks to 'madam' (who is not there) off-stage right, and to 'God' who seems to be in a crevice of the ceiling.*

She speaks sternly, as though always telling someone off – the habit of defending her eccentricity from mocking children, perhaps. She's never still, constantly moving, bringing articles out of her skirt to check and exchange for others in her 'old woman's bundle'. Between the words we hear, she mumbles.

---

* Sung by Richard Crook with the orchestra from 'Naughty Marietta' by Young and Herbert, available from BBC archives.

These are the actions of her scrubbing, they are meticulous:
rag into pail, slop water around area to be cleaned, rub huge
Lifebuoy soap onto huge scrubbing brush – scrub! Wring out
rag, make a length, draw length down bit by bit to gather
soapy area, squeeze out, draw length down again, and so on
until the final drying up with a wrung-out cloth.

The ritual satisfies her. When done she pours dirty water
down sink, fills it with fresh, places it on stove, a small light.

Spring 1939.

ANNIE. They tell me I smell. I don't smell nothing,
madam. But then no one don't know nothing about
themselves, do they? Lessun* they look in a mirror.
(*Idea.*) I'll look in one, shall I? Got one here.

> *Rummages among her numerous skirts.*

Somewhere.

> *Withdraws a chipped handbag mirror.*

Long time since I looked in a mirror. Don't tell you
much, 'cept you're growing old. That's all *I* see. I see
this face but I don't know anything about it, 'cept it's
growing old.

> *Raises mirror to her face.*

'Mornin', Annie Wobbler,' I say, 'mornin'.' Me talking
to myself that is. 'You're growing old, Annie Wobbler,'
I say, 'old! old!' Funny feeling looking at yourself and
not knowing what you see. So I don't do it much. Old!
What did I do to deserve that? Don't understand
nothing, me. (*Pause.*) I don't smell. (*Sniffs.*) I mean
that's not a smell, madam, that's me.

> *Puts away mirror, lowers leaf of kitchen cabinet,*

---

* unless

*rummages among her skirts, finds tin plate, tin mug,
and knife, places them on cabinet leaf, talking
meanwhile.*

She's very polite about it though, the madam. She ses
'You washed today, Annie?' I ses 'Course I did,
madam, course I did!' I don't know what she takes me
for.

They're Jew people. (*To 'God'.*) Your lot! They don't
do no Jew things like I've seen other Jew people do,
candles and prayers and straps round their arms, but
they're Jew people all the same. Like I don't do no
Christian things but I'm a Christian person all the
same.

Takes knife to stone steps, sharpens it.

No, I don't do no Christian things. (*To 'madam'.*) I'm a
sinner, madam, that's what I am, a sinner! (*To herself.*)
You're a sinner, Annie Wobbler, your mother would be
ashamed of you so it's thank-your-lucky-stars she's
dead-and-gone, thank them, thank them, go on thank
them! (*Beat.*) There! Now look what you've gone and
done. Made yourself cry, you stupid girl, you. You're a
dumb, stupid girl. Dumb!

Pause. Instant recovery.

'Bout time I had my tea, I think.

*She pours milk into cup, spoons tea from tea-caddy
into tea-strainer, but hesitates. Her alter-ego chides
her – she's put too much in. She retrieves a little back
into the caddy.*

Wonder what's in the cabinet. (*To 'God'.*) Madam said
I could help myself. (*To 'madam'.*) You're very kind,
madam. (*To 'God'.*) 'I trust you, Annie,' she said. 'We
don't have anything, besides.' (*Opens cabinet.*) She's

right! (*Taking them out.*) A little cheese, a little butter, some Jew bread. They don't have much more'n what I've got. (*To 'madam'.*) Lord knows how you can afford sixpence for a cleaning woman like me, madam. (*To 'God'.*) They can't.

> *She butters loaf, then cuts, holding bread to her bosom, sawing towards herself.*

She tell me 'We'll give you sixpence or some bread and tea. Whichever's around.' Fair enough. Scrub a couple of floors, flight of steps. Fair enough.

> *Reaches for a jar.*

What's this? Rollmops? I like rollmops. Madam says they're pickled herrings. (*To 'madam'.*) Pickled herrings to you, madam, rollmops to us! (*Unscrews jar, forks one out.*) You're very kind, madam. (*Bites.*) (*To 'God'.*) Funny people, foreigners.

> *She sits to her bread and butter. Folds slice, pulls out soft centre, stuffs crust in pocket.*

(*To 'God'.*)* For the birds.

Still, that's what comes of living in the East End. All sorts live here. You'd think because all sorts live here they'd leave you alone. But they don't, madam, they don't.

> *Kettle is boiling. She pours water over the tea leaves waiting in the strainer.*

Not the way *I* was taught to make tea. Never use twice-boiled water my first madam said, you boil the goodness away. Fresh water, heat the pot, a spoonful for each person, one for 'is knob, and then leave. Not like this.

---

* These stage directions will now be dropped, having given an indication of how she moves between 'God' and 'madam'.

Mug cupped in hands, she sips.

Funny people, foreigners.

Sips and eats.

You're very kind, madam.

I mean if I walked around Knightsbridge where I *used* to work, I'd understand. What's a girl like this doing up Knightsbridge my other madam would ask, for sure. But not 'ere, not 'ere in the East End. Everyone's common 'ere, madam, why should they stop *me*?

Imitates policeman.

'Where you off to then?'
'I'm off to do some work so leave me be.'
'You? Work? What work? Who for?'
'Cleaning for a respectable madam that's who for so you mind *your* business and I'll mind mine!' That upset him.
'You can't talk to me like that, missus, I'm an h'officer of the law and I've a right to stop and question who I please.' He was young so I forgive him, though why I should I don't know because the young is supposed to respect the old not that the old respect the young or the old respect the old or anybody any more respects anybody.
'What's your name?'
'Annie Wobbler,' I says. Defiant-like. 'Annie Wobbler!'
'Annie who?'
'Wobbler! Wobbler, Wobbler, Wobbler!' I get very angry when people make fun of my name, even before they start to make fun I get angry.
'Where did you get a name like that from?' he asks.
'I had a mother, didn't I, and a father? A good woman and a good man with a good name.'
'Funny name.'

'Oh?' I says. 'Funny?'

'Wobbler,' he says. And he wobbles. Like they all do. And you're supposed to laugh. They do, I don't!

'Funny names?' I tell 'im. 'I'll give you funny names. Mister Katz what doesn't like dogs! Mrs Smelly who washes too much! Miss Bubbles what burst! Mister Horse, and Hearse, and Lamb, and Sod, and Mrs Sore-At-Heart, and Mister D'Eath-At-Your-Door, and Mister Pain-In-The-Arse!' That shut him up a bit. 'Funny names?' I tell 'im. 'I'll give you funny names!'

Agitatedly she rises to wash mug and plate in sink.

Then he asks about my father. 'What's that to you?' I tell 'im.

'You interest me,' he says.

'Oh I do, do I?' My father! I don't remember what my father did. What did he want to go and ask me that for, madam. 'You've no right to ask me about my parents, that's no business of yours and not in your call of duty. My name's Annie Wobbler, I sleep at Rowton House and I work for my living doing for people. Now 'op it!'

Dries mug and plate with tea-cloth that's hanging on side of cabinet.

Who can remember? I think my father was a Frenchy. Mother, father, sisters, brothers. I had 'em all. Dead and gone. 'Cept this sister. Now *she* had money. Don't know where from – used to think some of it should have come my way – she never helped me is all *I* know. She tell me . . . She tell me the money . . . She tell me that the money . . . Now what did she tell me? (*Pause. Memory protects itself. Angrily.*) Oh, I don't know what she tell me. All I know is she 'ad a baby so I couldn't stay with 'er and that was that! (*Pause.*) Bright little youngster *he* was, madam, always said 'is prayers, but *she* weren't no good. 'Annie,' she says to me, 'you can

'ave something to eat and then you must go.' Well . . .
madam . . .

> *Tucks mug, plate and knife back into the folds of her*
> *skirt. Reaches for her bundle, sits on stool, opens*
> *bundle, sets aside old black shoes, brush and black*
> *polish; on the drop leaf she places two old tins. One she*
> *rattles, it has buttons in it; the other she opens, it has*
> *tobacco. From a pocket she draws out cigarette ends*
> *picked off the street.*

> *Throughout remaining passages she will polish her*
> *'best' over-polished shoes, and unpick cigarette ends to*
> *fill her tobacco tin.*

Not even photos left. Just faces. I see them. Who
knows, my father might even have been one of you Jew
people. So, one God's as good as another I say and I go
to synagogue on Saturdays and church on Sundays –
take no risks! (*Beat.*) You need a family.

Family. What'd he want to go and ask me that for?
Questions! Everybody asks questions. They all want to
know about you. Madam says 'Annie,' she says, 'Annie,
how did you get like this?' What a question.

> *Considers it. Gloom.*

Because I was a nothing, madam, and I knowed I was a
nothing. That's knowledge for you. I wasn't told, I
wasn't treated bad, but it came to me. Nothing! A
nothing Annie Wobbler! Nothing brains and nothing
looks and nothing grace. A serving-maid-for-other-
people. A bag of rags and bones. Sack of old coal, that
was me. (*Imitating coalman.*) 'Sack o' coal! Sack o'
coal!' They used to come on lorries, one man drivin',
another heavin' an' callin': 'Sack o'coal!' Got all the
parts wrong when they put me together. Needed to rub

me out and draw me again. (*Remembering.*) 'Sack o'
coal!' (*Beat.*) We was all young once, madam.

Abruptly, changing mood.

The first people I ever worked for was real good to me
they was. Down in Surrey. Forget the name of the
village, madam, but it *was* Surrey. Pretty. And a pretty
house. There was five bedrooms upstairs, a drawing
room downstairs, and a dining room, and a library 'cos
they was very high class and they read a lot, and
naturally a kitchen. Large! A large kitchen with a
whopping Aga cooker, and lots of brass pots on the
wall. But the rest of the house was modern, all modern.
The kitchen was old-fashioned but everywhere else was
full of new-fangled things. That's what the madam was
like. She no sooner see something in town than she'd
go on at the master begging and pleading and giving
him a dozen and one reasons why they should have it.
And they usually did. Very rich they were. But sweet,
and good-natured, always a kind word for the servants,
and sometimes a penny slipped in your hand.

And young. The madam was young. I used to look at
her and say 'You're very young to be a madam of a big
house like this.' And that used to make her laugh. 'I'm
not a madam,' she would say. 'A madam isn't always a
nice person. You *call* me madam but I'm *mistress* of the
house.' But I didn't understand what she was on about.
'You're the madam to me so I call you madam,' I tell
her, and that was that. (*Pause.*) Young. Both of us. Her
and me. And beautiful. I used to stare at her. Blue eyes
she had, I remember, and milky hair, and creamy skin.
Noble. She liked me staring at her, I could tell. Always
pretended she didn't know, but she knew, and I knew
she knew. Got to her when I was seventeen and stayed
eighteen months. Reckon I must have loved her.
Young. Both of us.

Abruptly, changing mood.

What did I leave for if they was so kind? Oh! I can't really remember, madam. I just felt – I don't know – I just felt I 'ad to leave. Go somewhere else. There was lots of places down in Surrey so finding work wasn't a problem and the madam give me a good reference, bless 'er. A very good reference as a matter of fact. I got it here, somewhere.

She stands, turns her back to audience, secretive, rummages in her skirts, takes out a bundle of letters, old, clumsily tied with string.

Look. All references. Kept them all. 'Cos y'see I couldn't ever stay in one place. I'd work a year, eighteen months and then 'ad to move. Don't ask me why, madam, I don't know why. I never knew why.

She's finished untying string. Looks through letters.

Here it is. The first reference I ever got. Cor! I haven't looked at this for years, not for years.

She extracts it, looks at it in silence as though reading it. Then –

I never could read. Nor write. Nor add. Nor dance. Nor talk proper. The master once tried to teach me to ride a bicycle but I never found the way to balance, and I hurt myself so many times I got frightened and give up. (*Returns to letter.*) But I *remember* what it said 'cos there was another girl there what read it to me again and again so I learned it and . . . (*Remembering.*) Yeah – this other girl. Cor! I'd forgotten her.

Now *she* got on. *She* had a strong nature. Tiny but – oooh, fierce! No bigger'n this she was, with green eyes and red 'air and energy like a steam engine. I used to *watch* her and get tired. 'Ere now, listen to this, madam.

She not only did all she was told, but she *invented* things what needed to be done. Bloody went around looking for them. Well, I wasn't doing that. I did what I was told, but if no one told I didn't do it. Not old redhead though. You looked at her and you knew, she was alive every minute of the day. Not like me, madam. Most of the day I'm dead. I'm dead or not there. Don't know where I go because when I come back I can't think where I've been. But the redheaded steam engine, she filled every second with thinking or asking or doing or planning – whew! *She* weren't made for service. 'You aren't made for service,' I tell her. 'No one's made for service,' she say, 'but you do have to start somewhere, don't you?' She started, *I* didn't! God all the parts wrong when they put me together. Needed to rub me out and draw me again.

Finally getting to letter.

'To whomever it may concern.' I used to love saying that to myself. 'To whomever it may concern. Annie Wobbler is a good and willing girl. She is completely trustworthy and will work for anyone who is kind to her.' Huh! All I did was tell the madam when the soap had gone small and when toilet paper was needed. 'To whomever it may concern.'

Abruptly changing mood.

Had to leave, though, madam. Always felt full of holes and had to leave. They left bits out when they put me together, see, so I couldn't never understand nothing, madam. All a foreign language to me. Nothing! A nothing Annie Wobbler! 'Sack o' coal! Sack o' coal!' (*Beat.*) 'To whomever it may concern.'

Ties up letters. Returns them under her skirt.

Still, this lot's good sorts. Poor. Very poor. Rollmops,

cheese, and a bit of Jew bread. That's poor. You can't get no poorer than that!

Begins to clear away bits and pieces from the drop leaf.

There's four of them. The master, the madam, the little master and the little madam. The little madam's older than the little master. He's seven, she's fifteen. And he's a right little (*Beat.*) master. (*In one breath.*) Effin' and blindin' and up and down these stairs and always with answers and his socks about his ankles and a tide mark where 'is face is washed and his neck isn't and his friends yellin' and his mother always chasin' and his father saying nothin' or not much more than nothin' – a right little master! I remember when he was born his grandmother took one look at him and said 'He's either going to be a great man or a murderer.' Well on the way to being a murderer I should think. Or murdered!

I nearly murdered him once. He come at my hat. Wanted it off. He stood over these railings here (*Enacts scene.*) as I was coming up the stairs, and he snatched. I got lots of needles in it so it didn't come away, but cor! did I jump and scream! 'My hat, my hat, my hat! No one's got the right to take my hat.' And I do believe my being upset made him upset, and my crying made him cry. 'You wear it all the time,' he tell me, 'we never see your head.' Well what does anyone want to see my head for? That's not a head anybody would want to see, is it? Besides, I tell him, if I want to keep my head to myself that's my right! That's *my* head, my head to do what I like with. Cover it, uncover it, smother it, cut it, perm it, dye it – what I like with it!

She's upset herself in remembering. Needs to recover.

I'm bald under this hat. Got no hair worth speaking of. What'd he wanna go and upset me like that for?

Returns to packing away bundle.

He upsets everyone sooner or later. But they all love him. That's the funny part of it. They all love him but no one can control him. 'Cept his sister. She controls him. He listens to her. Very clever girl she is. Wears a school uniform from the Spitalfields Foundation School. Talks posh. Says (*Blowing on each word.*) 'Hwhen. Hwhich. And hwhether.' She's got all the world on her, that one, he listens to her, she's noble. *She's* noble but *he's* bonkers! (*Rolls a newspaper into a funnel.*) I once come early and he was still in bed and he made a tent out of this big feather cushion, a 'deck' they call it, and he was inside with a piece of rolled newspaper sticking up out of the top, like a chimney, and he was speaking through it. 'This is the BBC Home Service. *The Man In Black.* Toot de toot, toot! Tonight's ghost story will be . . .' and then he'd tell this story to send shivers up you.

(*Rising.*) The BBC Home Service! *The Man In Black*! (*Little dance.*) Toot de toot, toot.

She moves sadly to the pail on the stove.

Gawn! Bloody all dried up! Have to fill it again.

Takes hold of handle.

Cor bloody blimey that's bleedin' hot, if you'll forgive my French. (*Nursing hand.*) Sod it! That hurt. As if I didn't have enough.

Takes a cloth and tries again. Fills pail with water, replaces it on stove. Regards hand. She's close to tears.

That'll bring a blister up, that'll bring a sodding blister up. Oh dear!

Sits. Mind wanders. Eyes glaze over. Dozes. Then – starts awake.

Hurrah! Hurrah! (*Pause.*) What did I say that for? What was I thinking of? (*Pause.*) Everyone's got a hurrah in them, Annie Wobbler. Even you used to say hurrah about something or other. But what?

Music: 'Ah, Sweet Mystery of Life'.

Hurrah! Hurrah! Doesn't even sound like my voice. 'Sack o' coal! Sack o' coal!' Hurrah! Hurrah!

Faint, sad echoes of a lost past.

Hold.

Then –

– with glazed eyes she slowly rises, walks downstairs, turns her back on the audience, secretive, as though doing something private. *

The set slowly changes.

She's unhooking her entire costume which –

– she throws aside, sweeping her hat with wig off from her head, revealing –

– a strong young woman with a mass of red hair who is –

PART TWO

Anna

ANNA, *a mass of flaming red hair, is in black underwear, black stockings and suspender belt.* ANNIE*'s black Victorian boots are not out of place.*

---

* In the London production the actress walked slowly down the stairs to the front of the set. Between the railings, where a bar is missing, sat a bowl which looked as though it contained cat's milk. It contained oil with which the actress washed off her make-up using the tea-cloth to wipe herself dry.

She moves forward into the new setting, takes a dress from off a full-length Victorian mirror, dances with it to the lilt of 'Ah Sweet Mystery of Life', hangs it on a hook on the wall, and, as music ends, stands triumphantly before the mirror.

ANNA. What *is* there about you?

> *She's full of fun, over-brimming with energy, the world is before her. But disturbing her sense of the future is a fear of what she might be leaving behind, that she may not be what she feels she* can *be.*

> *A leather stool sits before a Victorian dressing table on which is a typewriter, a small mirror, a box of cosmetics, and other props which will be needed in the next scene.*

> *We are in student digs. The place is London, the dialect Yorkshire – or anywhere north of Birmingham and south of Carlisle. The time is now.*

> ANNA *talks to her image in the tall mirror from wherever she is in the room.*

What *is* there about you?

It can't be your degree in French because he's got one in classics. It must be your breasts.

> *She pulls down straps, saucily, and ambles with sedate dignity back and forth.*

'She walks in beauty, like the night . . .' (*Halts. Deflates.*) And it would need to be night.

> *Places mirror in a more comfortable position.*

What is there about you? That trunk surely doesn't belong to those legs. I think I'd better go back to the shop and get them to sort this lot out, there's been a terrible mix-up here somewhere.

Attempts a Marilyn Monroe pose before the mirror. But gives up.

What *do* you think you're doing, Anna? And in black! My God! You're so corny. If he's going to want you it'll have to be for your mind, the power of your intellect. (*Beat.*) Perhaps I'd better stick to black underwear. No! You *have* got intellect. A first-class honours degree in French, translations to and from. (*Ripping sheet out of typewriter.*) Offenbach!

Recites to her image in mirror.

Ne suis-je donc rien?
Que la tempête de passions s'appaise vers toi!
L'homme n'est plus; renais poète!
Je t'aime, Hoffman. Appartiens-moi!

But what does it mean?
Now stop that, Anna. This tedious English habit of boasting ignorance. Three chaste and Cambridge years of slog – you know very well what it means. (*Still regarding herself in mirror.*) And take those absurd boots off.

Grabs leather stool, sits to take off boots, translating meanwhile.

'*Ne suis-je donc rien?*'
'Am I nothing?'
'*Que la tempête de passions s'appaise vers toi!*'
'Look how passion's tempests assuage around you . . .'
'*A*ssuage *a*round?' Bloody hell, Anna! (*Trying again.*)
'*S'appaise vers toi! S'appaise vers toi* . . .' Ah! '*Deflate* around you.' Good! So –
'Am I nothing? How the tempestous passions
Deflate around you . . .'
Oh good grief, Anna. Balloons and bladders deflate, not passions! Be free! Free! *R*ecreate the poem.

'And am I nothing? Look! Tempests and passions . . .'

Hesitant, then triumphantly –

'Blaze around you.
The man is no more! Take hold, poet,
I love you! Belong to me.'

Her boots are off.

That's better. Great stuff! They don't talk like that today. (*To the mirror.*) As the fat actor once said, 'You've got brains and black underwear? Flaunt them!'

She tries on an assortment of high-heeled shoes, regarding herself in the mirror and chatting meanwhile.

Why *don't* the English like cleverness? We produce enough. 'Long live the simple man!' 'Raw instinct!' 'Salt of the earth!' 'Knowledge destroys innocence!' Well there was nothing charming about *my* innocence, I can tell you. Perpetual bewilderment! Non-stop ignorance! Didn't know if I was coming or going. Even when I was coming – oops! Right, I said, must put a stop to all this. Goodbye innocence, you've had your time. Innocence is for the innocent, and those who shall remain innocent when that time is done shall be called stupid, and the wrath of the Lord shall be upon them. Get thee with knowledge or thou wilt be got with child and an office job.

Stands to regard herself in the mirror. Will this pair of shoes match?

So here I am. Educated!

She struts as though at a cocktail party, shaking hands, nodding, bowing.

And I shall *not* go naked into those literary cocktail parties, nor the political salons nor the intimate dinners of erudite dons and heavyweight novelists, for I am armed with a set of cultural references which sparkle like a tiara of diamonds and announce to one and all who I am and the stuff of which I am made.

Coquettishly accepts an imaginary light to an imaginary cigarette from an imaginary, tall, dark stranger.

Thank you!

Catches herself in the mirror. Deflates.

But who are *you*? I've never seen *you* here before. Do you always go shopping like that? (*Pause.*) What *is* there about you? It can't be your body because it's kind of odd! It can't be your black suspenders because he hasn't seen them yet. (*Pause.*) It must be an alchemy of the right mistakes which, against all the odds, combines to produce what they call *je ne sais quoi*! (*Beat.*) And neither does anybody else.

Tries on another pair of shoes.

On the other hand maybe the English think scholarship should conduct itself modestly. Unlike black underwear! Maybe they can't bear whorish scholars who parade like over-fleshed tarts in the corridors of academe. Ah! Perhaps that's what there is about you – you're not a scholar at all, you're an over-fleshed tart!

Yes you bloody are a scholar! First-class honours degree in French! Against all the cultural odds! (*Calling out.*) You hear that, Mother, you old Domesday Book you? Your daughter's got a degree in froggy-talk! Tell that to Aunty Maud and all the others in 'Coronation Street'. I've got brains and black underwear and I'm not ashamed. I-am-not-ashamed! (*Referring to her shoes.*) Yes! These!

*She sits before her dressing table and begins laying out
her make-up.*

The trouble is *he's* also clever. Difficult. *He* can be
modest about his cleverness but *I* will have to hide
mine, I can see. Why *don't* men like their women to be
clever? They like them to be clever but not cleverer
than them. Still, I don't suppose anybody enjoys
anybody being cleverer than them. It's so undemo-
cratic.

Where's my black liner? What did I do with my black
liner? Who has nicked my bloody black liner? What's
the good of having black suspenders against my lily-
white thighs if I've got no black liner for my lily-white
eyes? (*Peering into small mirror.*) What lily-white eyes?
How can I lengthen my saucers, darken my mystery,
deepen my *weltschmerz*? You mean 'melancholy' don't
you? Then say 'melancholy' instead of all this foreign
gibberish. You're English and living in England and we
prefer straight plain honest-Jane talk and calling a
spade a spade and besides no one knows what it means
and where's my fucking eye-liner? Ah! (*Finds it.*) Nearly
had to call it off.

*Now all her bits and pieces are assembled ready for the
long ritual. She begins. After a while –*

What *is* there about you? I mean *that* is a face? The
peak and epitome of feminine beauty? Look at that
nose. Grafted on at the last minute from a mythological
Greek. Clytemnostril! And that mouth! It's so full of
teeth it's bitten my lips away. And look at those teeth.
Well there isn't anything else to look at is there? And
that chin! What chin? I don't see a chin. (*Across to her
image in the long mirror.*) Do you see a chin? I see a
neck, I see a face, but it's all one to me. And those eyes!

Eternally praying! I mean nothing, but nothing is right is it? And yet (*Drawing herself up in profile.*) there is a kind of haphazard beauty there. A kind of accidental splendour. A kind of gargoylian loveliness. (*Beat.*) At least nothing that a little bit of black liner can't put right.

> *Continues to make up. We are witnessing an amazing transformation.*

He says he can't bear women who make up. (*Beat.*) Tough shit! (*Beat.*) Anna, you're coarse. And perverse. If he'd've said he loved made-up women you'd've gone plain wouldn't you? (*Quoting him.*) 'I mean I don't object to the quantity you've got on now, but in excess of that . . .' (*Beat.*) I wasn't wearing any fucking make-up! Anna, Anna! Old women can't wear short skirts, nor can educated ones cling to their cosy gutters.

> *She concentrates on her make-up, compelling to watch. After a while –*

Silenced yourself haven't you? Think what you're going to do to him then. (*Pause.*) I know, what about . . . what about listing the things you don't like about him. That way he'll be a pleasant surprise.

He talks loudly. As though he's more interested to impress the strangers nearby rather than the stunning woman before him, and that I find mightily offensive as well as embarrassing.

He constructs his sentences like a bad Victorian novel. (*Quoting him.*) 'Yes! I have! I have read the entire *Divina Commedia* of Dante, and what is more – though it becomes me not to say it, but what I say is that only the *faint*-hearted are modest and God forbid I should be quoted among *their* number – what is more I've read it in Italian! Not, I might add, if I must be truthful – and I must for I'd be loath to have you think me a fibster or dissembler – not that *all* its subtleties and nuances made themselves known to me, still, no small achievement, notwithstanding, for one so very English and reared to believe that all art the other side of the Channel was high-falutin' codswallop!'

Well, more or less. And those long sentences. I find myself holding my breath and unable to put the next spoonful of crème brulée into my mouth which stays open and ugly and makes people stare at me and Jesus Christ he's got me constructing them now!

He eats too quickly. *And* noisily. *And* insensitively. And he *insists* on everything. 'Might I suggest the little-known *poussin à la grec* which I *insist* you try and which I guarantee will do things undreamt-of to your taste buds the sensitivity of which will hereafter be offended by anything coarse. One *poussin à la grec*, waiter, which the young lady would like with creamed spinach and sauté potatoes – trust me!' *C'était dégueulasse!* The Greeks don't bother with fucking poussins! Restaurants like that *cater* for the gullible like him.

And he's so nice with everybody. I told him: 'You're unbearable! You like everyone!' 'My goodness and fiddle-de-de,' he says, 'And what's wrong with that, pray?' He actually did say 'pray'. 'It's not *that* you like everyone,' I told him, 'it's what that implies.' 'Oh, and would it be too much to request of you an explanation of what it is that's implied?' (*Talking like a Victorian Gothic novel.*) 'Yes,' I retorted, my nostrils flaring, my bosom heaving, and my heart pounding for the fray, 'if you like people it means you don't envy them enough to dislike them, and what right have you to be so confident that nothing arouses your envy? There's nothing in *me* you envy, dammit! That's terrible! That's insulting! It's so damn arrogant of you!' I could see he understood nothing. (*Beat.*) Nothing! (*Beat.*) Nothing!

And I'm convinced he quotes from books he's never read or don't exist.

And he dances like a broomstick.

And he doesn't like Barbra Streisand.

And, Jesus Christ, he doesn't make me laugh! What *am* I going on this date for?

> *Aware of herself now fully made-up and ravishing. With mounting triumph –*

Because – he's your first date since becoming a BA first-class honours and your cultural references shine like diamonds and you've broken the stranglehold of those century-old genes of crass ineptitude and supplication and you've unknown muscles to flex and a lot of intimidating to make up for and he's just the size and texture your teeth need sharpening upon.

> *Grabs dress and holds it to herself before the mirror.*

Upon which your teeth need sharpening.

> *Puts it on.*

Upon which your teeth need!

Upon which!

> *Stands tall before the mirror. She is stunning.*

What *is* there about you?

> *Music: 'Ah, Sweet Mystery of Life'.*
>
> *Fade to half light.*
>
> *The set slowly changes.*

She unhitches dress beneath which is another, flings off her wig of red hair, to become –

PART THREE

Annabella Wharton – One

Aged forty-one, a novelist, in her new penthouse flat. She is dressed with intellectual as opposed to chic elegance. Beneath ANNA*'s red wig is revealed a severe bun.*

ANNABELLA *is preparing for something. She folds the mirror to become a tapestry, an object she places somewhere, as a stand-in for someone.*

Who? What is about to happen?

A VOICE-OVER,* *a woman's, hard and brittle, echoing as though she's imagining it, is heard asking a question.*

VOICE-OVER. Miss Wharton, this is your fourth novel and, unlike the others, it's a phenomenal success. Instalments in the *Sunday Times*, translated into fourteen languages, the film rights sold for a quarter of a million dollars, the subject of controversy in the heavyweight literary journals. Annabella Wharton, what does it feel like being Annabella Wharton today?

> *She seems to be deciding how to answer, which persona to adopt.*

> *Is she rehearsing for an interview?*

ANNABELLA. Oh well, oh, well – er – to be honest . . .

Blackout.

---

* Both VOICE-OVERS should be recorded by the actress.

ACT TWO

Annabella Wharton – One

VOICE-OVER. Miss Wharton, this is your fourth novel and, unlike the others, it's a phenomenal success. Instalments in the *Sunday Times*, translated into fourteen languages, the film rights sold for a quarter of a million dollars, the subject of controversy in the heavyweight literary journals. Annabella Wharton, what does it feel like being Annabella Wharton today?

ANNABELLA. Oh well, oh, well – er – to be honest . . .

After hesitation she decides on her persona: modest, self-effacing, bewildered.

She puts half-glasses on her nose. Too high. Pushes them down.

. . . not much different, I'm afraid.

Not bad. That's a voice will amuse them . . .

You'll still find me going up the road to buy fish and chips for my dinner some nights.

. . . an attitude they'll warm to.

Not much of a cook. Never was. Not that I don't like good food. As Doctor Johnson says: 'He who doesn't mind his belly will hardly mind anything else!' But other people's good food. The kitchen confuses me, see. Never know what to reach for first. I mean you watch me fry an egg and you'd laugh. Burn the butter, crack the eggs before I've got the pan out, forget the toast, miss the plate. I mean really, I find the material things of this world a bit double-Dutch, so I can't quite understand the meaning of a quarter of a million dollars. It's a bit of a lark, if you ask me, isn't it? A lark! I mean – quarter of a million!

Now where's that bottle of whisky. You will have a drink won't you? 'Fraid whisky's all I've got, it's all I drink. Can't really bring myself to buy anything else. Not very polite of me, I know, ought to think of my friends and all those other visitors who come, but, well, I get into the off-licence and I look at all that array of bottles and think I can't choose from that lot, take me all day, and they're all synthetic, know what I mean? Concocted! Contrived! Experimental! Not like whisky. Whisky was always there wasn't it?

She finds bottle, and offers.

No? Oh well, I will. Need it. Cheers.

Drinks.

Besides, my accountant looks after things like money, and I tell him 'It's your job, your decision, you work out what's best and tell me what to do and I'll do it.' So he's opened an account in Switzerland and it gathers interest, and every so often I go over there and fill my pockets and come home and pay my bills, and then I can attend to my writing. Fairyland I call it. Four times a year I hop on a plane to fairyland and that's about the extent of my travelling!

Hate travelling. The Brontës didn't need to travel and it suits me. I agree with Doctor Johnson you know, who, according to Boswell agreed with the Lord Essex who advised the Earl of Rutland 'rather to go an hundred miles to speak with one wise man, than five miles to see a town'.

And I'm not sure I'd go five miles to speak to a wise man either.

(*Singing.*) 'And as for fortune and as for fame . . .' Ha! I don't *feel* famous, I don't think I even comprehend the nature of fame. I mean I *know* I'm famous because people like you keep wanting to interview me and *tell* me I'm famous, but I don't actually know what I'm supposed to feel. Doesn't alter my conversation. I still can't talk at dinner parties or be witty or tell stories. I tell stories but I tell them badly. Forget the punch-line or deliver it clumsily or get worked up in the middle instead of the end. And everybody else I know who writes seems to write better than I do, so I really don't understand any of it. Here today and gone tomorrow. Will *you* come wanting to interview me if my next novel doesn't receive such favourable attention? Of course you won't! And I don't blame you. It's not really talent that's important is it? I mean lots of writers are talented but not all that many sell their work for quarter of a million dollars, so it's silly and nonsense and a bit of a lark. (*Confidentially.*) I'm what's called a mid-culture writer. I give people the *impression* I'm treating them intellectually without actually calling their intellect into play. People feel much more comfortable with that sort of work which is why I've got all this attention. So there it is. That's how Annabella Wharton feels today, it's how Annabella Wharton felt yesterday, and, with God's grace and a bit of luck that's how Annabella Wharton will feel tomorrow.

VOICE-OVER. Could you say what drives you to write?

ANNABELLA. Oh my goodness me, no. Oh good Lor, no. Drives me to write? *Drives* me to write? Nothing *drives* me to write. I just potter around you might say. Doodle. Start at the top of the page and work down. I'm not driven, I'm (*Beat.*) *used*! I start to create a character and suddenly – flip! There I am, dangled by him, or her, or it, puppet-like, made to do this then that then the other.

> *Reaches for her novel. Reads aloud. In the process her tone changes, becomes serious, absorbed by her prose.*

'It was the coldest day of the year. A desperate, cold, lonely day when lonely women commit cold and desperate acts they regret. Sarah Newman would regret this day, it was certain, that.'

(*To herself.*) '*It was certain, that*'? (*Reflecting.*) I didn't really need the word 'that'.

> *Returns to sending-up journalist.*

There! When I put pen to paper to write those first three words 'It was the', I didn't know the next word was going to be 'coldest'. It could have been 'hottest'. And if it had been 'hottest' then the rest of this prize-winning novel *The Speechless Sick* would have gone differently.

'It was the hottest day of the year. A defiant, rich and vibrant day when defiant women step out in control of their lives. Sarah Newman . . .'

Etc. etc.! And I didn't know her name would be Sarah Newman, either. Where did *that* come from? You ask me! I couldn't tell you. And I didn't know she was going to be desperate and lonely either, poor thing. And so there I am, having to write about a lonely and desperate woman named Sarah Newman. I didn't *want* to write about a lonely and desperate woman named Sarah Newman. I'd actually decided that morning to start a novel about Mary Magdalene! Tossed about!

Hooked! Dangled! Used! I'm not responsible for what I write, good Lor, no! Merely the medium through which they bring themselves to life. 'Not I! Not I! But the wind that blows through me', as D.H. Lawrence said, and many have agreed since.

VOICE-OVER. Are you saying that no themes drive you, you've no wish to communicate a –

ANNABELLA. Don't say it! Terrible word! A message? God forbid! Messages? They'd have my guts for garters. On the other hand . . . on the other hand . . . if anybody needs to see something *in* my novels, fine! Very good! Glad to have been of service. That's their prerogative to interpret, take what they want, what they need. A good piece of literature is open to many interpretations, which is what I intend. As Doctor Johnson or someone said: the smaller a work of art, the greater should be the co-efficient of expansion. God forbid I should mean *one* thing. Good Lord, no! I would like my work to be approached as one does a crossword puzzle. Clues! I give clues. That's what I write, a collection of clues. (*Confidentially.*) Actually, to be honest, between thee and me, I just think I've been lucky to have struck a rather rich vein of contemporary stupidity!

VOICE-OVER. Perhaps we ought to go back to the beginning and ask how and when did you begin writing.

ANNABELLA. Chinese poetry! Began with Chinese poetry! When I was fifteen and swotting for my mock exams I used the local reference library, one of those huge buildings harbouring statues of writers and thinkers from Cicero to Carlyle so beloved of those earnest Victorians, and among the books I discovered was one – an anthology of world poetry. (*Reaches from*

among books scattered over sofa.) There was Latin poetry,
yes, we'd done one or two of those; and Greek poetry,
no, but not surprising, we'd heard the Greeks were
once a great civilisation; the Hebrews – the Hebrews?
Oh yes, they'd written the Bible and parts of that
counted as poetry. But then – Sanskrit? Japanese?
Chinese? *Chinese*? The Chinese wrote poetry?

I don't know why that should have struck me as
improbable since I now know that everyone, everywhere, all the time has written poetry, but for some
strange reason it came as a revelation or to use the
current jargon, a culture shock. And *what* poetry! So
simple, so everyday, so delicate. I began at once to
write Chinese poetry. By the time the evening was over
I'd written half a dozen, by the time the week was
through I'd filled half a school exercise book, and
within a year I'd a whole volume ready for instant
publication. I was launched! Or rather – struck! From
that moment on I became a compulsive scribbler.
Everything I saw, heard, experienced went echoing
round my head and became inexorably metamorphosed
into literature: prose! a line of dialogue! Chinese poetry!

> The leaves fall dead at my feet.
> I walk home through them thinking of my tea.
> I know it is autumn.
> In the front room there is a fire.
> On the kitchen table are bangers and baked
>   beans . . .

Easy, thoughtless. Began with Chinese poetry and now
no one's safe from encounters with me.

VOICE-OVER. Am I right in thinking you've been
married once?

ANNABELLA. Good Lor, no! Never! Couldn't conceive
of a man who'd want to share my scatty life. Unless

he'd be prepared to cook for me and generally keep house. I did live with a man once, for three years. I don't really know whatever happened to him. He kind of evaporated away. After a few weeks I just realised that he wasn't there any more.

VOICE-OVER. Do you have any children?

ANNABELLA. I don't think so.

VOICE-OVER. You once said you write in your head. How do you remember it all?

ANNABELLA. Diary! I keep a diary. Every day. My obsession. I've got fifty volumes. Constantly dip into them.

VOICE-OVER. Do you have any bêtes noires?

ANNABELLA. Not really. I think everything's a bit bête-noirey once you get under the surface.

VOICE-OVER. You have no fears?

ANNABELLA. Oh good Lor, yes. Everything frightens me. The morning, the doorbell, the telephone, interviewers, fish-on-the-bone, the post, Doctor Johnson . . .

VOICE-OVER. Do you feel you have an endless flow of material?

ANNABELLA. . . . quarrelling cats, aeroplanes, ships, cars, bicycles, prams, politicians, mushrooms. . . .

VOICE-OVER. Do you feel you have an endless flow of material?

ANNABELLA. . . . heights, crowds, open spaces, closed spaces, three-point plugs, unboiled water, television news, Ayatollahs . . .

VOICE-OVER. But do you feel you have an endless flow of material?

ANNABELLA (*fiercely*). I really do feel I've had enough of questions for today. Thank you.

> *The interview is over. Her eyes hold contempt. Then –*
>
> *She relaxes and a great change comes over her, of sadness, it seems, for the performance she has just now put up.*
>
> *She walks to a pile of books on the cabinet, opens one to begin signing them. Has no will to. Reaches for a cigarette. The questions come at her again.*
>
> *The second persona she adopts is tense, tough, a withering, witty intelligence.*

Annabella Wharton – Two

VOICE-OVER (*a woman's. Eager, gushing*). Miss Wharton, this is your fourth novel and, unlike the others, it's a phenomenal success. Instalments in the *Sunday Times*, translated into fourteen languages, the film rights sold for a quarter of a million dollars, the subject of controversy in the heavyweight literary journals. Annabella Wharton, what does it feel like being Annabella Wharton today?

> *Long, long pause.*

ANNABELLA. Fucking Empress of China! (*Beat.*) Well you did ask.

VOICE-OVER. Seriously now.

> *Long, long pause.*

ANNABELLA. Fucking Empress of China! Nothing like

it! High! I'm high all the time. To come to that dinner-table throbbing with power from those detestable powerful people and have them begin to treat you with respect – nothing like it! It's cleansing, as though before – you were diseased, and now you're cured. The test is passed. Accepted! *You* know that *they* know that nothing can topple you now and that you can come and go and buy and match their extravagance-parading-as-generosity and oh! there-is-nothing-like-it!

Does this shock you? This is the kind of thing you're looking for isn't it?

Everything comes to you. Suddenly your past is unique. Suddenly your private life is fascinating. Suddenly you're photogenic, you're intelligent, you're an oracle, the look in your eye is feared. All that you've been saying for years that seemed presumptuous, misplaced, ill-conceived, and was greeted with bemused and mocking raised eyebrows, now appears wise, signifi-cant, valuable. 'Ah, this one knows what she's about and the world she's in.' Suddenly you're what the Irish call – a mensch!

But most gratifying is that suddenly you've become a magnet! For offers of work, for interviews, for chat programmes, charity appeals, lectures, articles, com-ments on the latest political crises or blunder, invita-tions to parties, a magnet for men! Oh, for those men of superb intellect – and smutty appetites!

And the awful thing is – it makes your lovely, neurotic, struggling, bohemian, former-self feel such a nonentity. A nothing! There she goes, weeping into the shadows, I don't need her, I don't know her. I glow with achievement. I blossom with arrival. I radiate, and I'm ravishing and would change with no one.

She reaches for a hand-mirror to check her make-up.

Empress of fucking China! No one!

VOICE-OVER. I see. Could you say what drives you to write?

ANNABELLA (*still gazing into hand-mirror*). Fame Money and Power, I think.

VOICE-OVER. No, seriously now.

ANNABELLA. Why do you imagine I'm *not* being serious? I write so that when I walk into a party there's a buzz, I'm looked at, regarded, wondered at. I write to be recognised in shops when I sign a cheque, on streets, at first nights. I write because artists who are successful are adored with a very special passion I find my soul needs like a drug.

VOICE-OVER. Are you saying that no themes drive you, no wish to communicate a –

ANNABELLA. – a message? Messages, said a Hollywood film producer, are for Western Union! I tell stories. They're long, they're rich, they're true, and those who have read them tell me they're spell-binding. Themes are for Ph.Ds and the Germans. As Doctor Johnson has observed: 'Mankind have a great aversion to intellectual labour', and I for one have no wish to redirect such a powerful aversion since it wouldn't buy me the house of my dreams, besides.

You're about to say you find that cynical. You probably think that everything I've said so far is cynical. Not true. I simply try to be honest. I'd like to present you (*Briefly imitating the first* ANNABELLA.) a modest, humble personality. But that's not, I'm afraid, the way I feel. I can't cope with men's stupidities and endless cruelties, and so I'm contemptuous of all but a few very extraordinary people about whom I care passionately, from whom I can take anything, and whose wisdom –

and motives – I trust totally. My loyalties are reserved for them. Now, criticise me, flaw me, despise me even, but you will never be able to write about me as a humbug.

How we doing? Is your tape working? The numbers of interviewers I've had who've put in their blank tapes and taken out their blank tapes.

VOICE-OVER. Perhaps we ought to go back to beginnings and ask how and when did you begin writing.

ANNABELLA. Ah! How and when! Well, let's see. There were two stages, actually. First – dreadful poems and dreadful stories and then – well, it happened like this.

Looks through filing cabinet.

I had an uncle. Worked as a sub-editor on the *Daily Mirror*. He also wanted to write. Had some short stories printed in a London evening newspaper, couple of plays on radio, that sort of thing. But nothing more. I used to type my first poems on his typewriter.

Finds a file containing a letter.

And this uncle grew old and cynical like lots of people do, and turned first to psychology and then to religion, and it was during his psychology period that one day I received a letter from him. (*Finds it.*) Momentous! He kept to himself most of the time, see, and when he *did* attend family do's his greatest pleasure was to adopt an aloof tone to any discussion that took place. So this letter, this letter was remarkable, remarkable for its absence of any cynicism whatsoever.

'Dear Annabella,' it said. He came from Wales.

She assumes a Welsh accent. 'Sings' the rhythm in the letter.

'Dear Annabella, I have something to reveal which I assure you will be beneficial to your future. Come and see me. Mornings usually will do. Yours, Uncle Dems. PS Keep this under your hat from the rest of the family.'

What could it be? It could be anything. Anything! A thousand pounds, perhaps, from insurance, which he wanted to give me so's I could take a year off from work to write my first novel. Thrilling! It was a thrilling letter! A remarkable, thrilling letter.

So I got up early next day to get to him early so's I wouldn't be late for work – I was working in a vinegar factory at the time – and my aunt let me in. Uncle Dems was still in bed.

'Oh no, I can't tell you. I've got cold feet. Forget it.'
'But Uncle Dems,' I say, 'I've got up specially early to come and see you. You might as well tell me now I'm here.'
'Oh, all right,' he says, 'I'll *tell* you why I asked you to come. I've been watching you,' he says. 'Over the years I've been watching you and I've come to the conclusion that I understand you. I understand you very well indeed. No one else in the family does, and no one else in the family would tell you what I'm going to tell you. But *I* will because I *do*. Now,' he says, 'you're not a very happy young woman. You're a good sort, intelligent, but you're confused. And it's perfectly understandable. Perfectly! Your parents quarrelled and you loved them both and you've got a conflict raging inside you which is giving you complexes that'll destroy you unless you have them seen to.'
'Complexes, Uncle Dems? What complexes?'
'Delusions of grandeur!'
'Delusions of grandeur?!!'
'Delusions of grandeur! *You* want to be a writer. You'll

never be a writer. Not in a hundred years, never! But there it is, this drive in you to compensate.

'And there's more. You're not a very imposing young woman and so you want to make up for it. Unhappy childhood, dimunitive figure – classical! *I'm* small and *I* wasn't happy either, and it affects people in different ways. Some want to be boxers, others want to be tycoons, some want to be Napoleon and some want to be writers! And the world is full of unhappy people who are little people and there's only one Napoleon and one Rockefeller and one Tolstoy –'
'Was Tolstoy small?' I asked him.
'Never in a hundred years will you publish a novel,' he said. 'I'll bet a hundred to one – your shilling to my five pounds,' he said, 'you'll never have a book published. And if you do, what then? You'll have to write another. And maybe, maybe that'll be published and your standard of living will go up and you'll have to write another and another and another, for fifty years – assuming you'll live to seventy-five which God willing I hope you will and longer – for fifty years you'll be expected to turn out books. Non-stop! Because you know,' he whispered it to me, 'you know that if you're silent for longer than two years out come those articles "Whatever happened to Annabella Wharton?" or "What and who were Annabella Wharton's enemies of promise?" I know,' he said, 'I've subbed them for the Sundays. And they're lethal. The world of literature,' he warned me, 'is vituperative, snake-infested, full of academics and half-educated commentators trying to be Doctor Johnson. Fifty years! And can you honestly tell me you've got all those books inside you? Can you? Psychiatry!' he counselled. 'There's the answer to your tears. Go and see a psychiatrist. He'll cure you of your delusions of grandeur. And that's what I have to tell you!'

No thousand pounds! But I was determined to win that fiver. And I did.

VOICE-OVER. You once said you write in your head. How do you remember it all?

ANNABELLA. I keep a diary, don't I!

VOICE-OVER. For posterity or insurance?

ANNABELLA. Oh, insurance! I listened well to Uncle Dems' warnings. And they're all hand-written so's when the time comes they'll have a value as original manuscripts *and* copyright material for publication. As you can see, I trust no one. I'm building the most formidable castle I can against the vicissitudes of the outside world in general, and the certain betrayal of my public in particular.

VOICE-OVER. Yes, I can see. I am right in thinking you've been married once?

ANNABELLA. Three times, actually. I've never mentioned the first two – they were nonentities and I felt rather ashamed to be caught ever having wanted such men. Now I feel strong and confident enough to own up to them.

VOICE-OVER. Do you have any children?

ANNABELLA. At least four.

VOICE-OVER. Do you have any bêtes noires?

ANNABELLA. Yes, people who sign petitions, attend conferences and lecture on the meaning of art.

VOICE-OVER. You have no fears?

ANNABELLA. Not now. None!

The interview is over. Her eyes hold contempt. Then –

She relaxes and a great change comes over her, of sadness it seems for the performance she had just now to put up.

She's tired of play-acting.

She's tired.

Tired.

She collects the pile of her books, brings them down to her desk to sign. Signs one. The light has faded. She moves to switch on a lamp-standard.

The questions come at her again. Both voices. Insistent. She cannot bear them. Rushes to her cabinet for a sheet of paper, down to her typewriter, as though creativity will get rid of the questioning.

Annabella Wharton – Three

The VOICES *of the first two interviewers echo out the first question again.*

VOICES.
Miss Wharton, this is your fourth novel and . . .

Miss Wharton this is your fourth novel and . . .
unlike the others it is a phenomenal success . . .

unlike the others it is a phenomenal success. . . .
. . . Annabella Wharton, what is it like being Annabella Wharton today?

She can't write. Angrily snatches paper out of typewriter. Knocks her books to the floor. Knows she must control her agitation.

ANNABELLA. 'Questioning,' said Doctor Johnson, 'is not the mode of conversation among gentlemen!'

Drops to her knees to collect fallen books.

'It is assuming a superiority, and it is particularly wrong to question a man concerning himself. There may be,' he said, 'parts of his former life which he may not wish to be made known to other persons, or even brought to his own recollection.'

Doctor Johnson! Not altogether true, I must admit. Sometimes *I* find myself with people so full of conversation and opinion and a retelling of their lives that I crave for one tiny question to be addressed to me. Eminently quotable, Doctor Johnson, *and* contradictable.

> *From here on* ANNABELLA *asks the questions herself, but still holding an imaginary exchange with the object standing in for 'the interviewer'.*

What does it feel like being Annabella Wharton today?

I'm not sure I can answer that. (*Tries hard.*) 'What does it feel like? Feel like?' Well, I'm gratified. Yes. I think I can safely say that. And I'm – relieved. Yes. That too. And I'm – well, well, to be honest (*Rises to take books back to cabinet.*) I think it's a rather fatuous question. (*Beat.*) If you'll forgive me.

> *She begins to unpin her hair.*

Could you say what drives you to write?

> *She searches painfully for the inexplicable. After a very long silence –*

No.

Am I saying no theme drives me, no wish to communicate a message?

(*Thoughtfully.*) People say they don't like messages. What do you think they mean? Do you think they'd rather the rose didn't tell them it was red? Or that people's eyes didn't speak? Or that there was never any writing on the wall? (*Pause.*) People are very odd, don't you think?

Or do you think they mean something else? 'Yes we all know expressions convey a message but please, only those we want to hear, the old ones, you know, like "death is the great leveller", or "love is blind", or that one about – how does it go now – "all men are equal".'

> *She begins to unhook stockings and, with her back to the audience, unhooks black underwear so that she can in one go peel off underwear and dress turning to reveal a vulnerable middle-aged woman in bra and panties by the end of the next section.*

One of the crassest utterances was uttered by a Hollywood film producer who said 'Anyone wants to send a message they use Western Union', while he himself spent millions on films communicating some of the most banal, shallowly felt, glibly expressed messages about life and death, crime and punishment, good and evil, love and hate, patriotism, nationalism, capitalism, liberty – *you* name it, *he* misrepresented it.

> *She puts on her dressing gown.*

Nevertheless, I try. I promise you I try to say nothing. Every morning I sit down at my desk I say 'Annabella,' I say, 'remember! Say nothing!' And there I sit, working hard to say nothing. Every novel I write has on the front page of the manuscript: 'There is no significance to this story whatsoever. Any resemblance between this story and meaning is purely coincidental.'

You say you write in your head. How do you remember it all?

A notebook for notes. A diary for the truth. In the notebook I write: 'Today my son pissed on me.' In the diary I write: 'As one grows older one becomes more fascist! Fight it.'

Perhaps we ought to go back to beginnings and ask how and when did you begin writing.

> *Trying hard to remember.*

There was a conversation I couldn't finish. Then! Was it then I began? (*Pause.*) Let's try again. There was a conversation I finished but wasn't satisfied with. Then? Was it then I began? (*Thinks again.*) Was I in love with my English teacher? 'Inexpressible love'? 'The shame of silence'? (*Pause.*) I think I began writing when I wanted to affect others the way writers affected me.
I think.

(*Fiercely.*) You know, bad prose is like toffee in your mouth – the vowels fall back to front and the consonants prick like splinters, and your jaw seems to ache.

That really didn't have anything to do with anything did it?

'How and when.'

(*Rising.*) Would you like some whisky? Or gin? Or vodka? Or brandy perhaps? I've a full cupboard somewhere of so much, I've forgotten what I *have* got.

> *A need to explain – desperate, urgent.*

It began with poetry. Why *is* it that a certain selection of words arranged in a certain way explode in you and yet, change one word, one syllable and there's not even a damp spark?

> *Moves to retrieve her poems from a cabinet-drawer, throws them around as she speaks.*

I keep getting this urge, you see, to write poetry. It's a very strong urge and I become filled with a special kind of . . . kind of . . . how can it be described? A kind of incorporeal expectation. A bit like being on heat. And out it comes, this poetry, this selection of words and images I *think* is poetry. And it's shit. And a pain. Such a pain. You've no idea the pain it is to begin with this heat, this fever, this sense that an astonishing assembly is about to take place and all that assembles is shit! Listen:

> Well, world, you have kept faith with me,
> Kept faith with me.

Miraculous, aren't they? Thomas Hardy. Simple, but! a magic assembly. Now –

> World world, you have kept faith with me . . .

Not quite the same is it.

> Well world, you've kept your faith.
> Kept your faith.

Not really.

> Well, world with me your faith was kept
> Your faith was kept.

I don't think so.

> Well, world, you have kept faith with me,
> Kept faith with me;
> Upon the whole you have proved to be
> Much as you said you were.

(*Achingly.*) To be a poet . . .

From her cabinet she finds cream and cotton-wool. It is time to remove the make-up from her face.

She moves down to her desk and her mirror.

How many times married?

Once! To a man who was drawn by the heat but left . . .

Do I have any children?

A son. Who pisses on me.

Do I have any bêtes noires?

People who quote Dr Johnson.

You have no fears?

Of being afflicted with a sense of futility. Of violence and certitudes. Of failing my son. Of being disliked . . . mediocre. (*Pause.*) Somewhere within us all is a body waiting to give up, don't you think?

Do you feel you have an endless flow of material?

My father used to have a 78 record of a song called 'Ah! Sweet Mystery of Life', and he'd put it on and it would get stuck at the 'myst'. (*Gently sings it.*) 'Ah sweet myst . . . sweet myst . . . sweet myst . . .' And then he'd push it and you'd get to 'life'. Well, I'm a bit like that. Stuck in the 'myst'.

'Ah sweet myst . . . sweet myst . . . sweet myst . . . sweet myst . . . sweet myst . . . sweet myst . . . sweet myst . . .'

> *Music: 'Ah Sweet Mystery of Life'.*
>
> *Lights slowly fade.*

Four Portraits – of Mothers

A set of vignettes

Four Portraits – of Mothers was first written for the Tokyo Festival of One-act Plays. It was first performed on 2 July 1982 at the Mitzukoshi Royal Theatre, Tokyo, by Michiko Otsuka, directed by Tsunetoshi Hirowatari. Its United Kingdom premiere took place during the Edinburgh Festival on 20 August 1984 at the Netherbow Theatre, Edinburgh, when it was performed by Anne Lacey, directed by Donald Smith. The first London performance was on 20 October 1987 at the Half Moon Theatre, given by Anne Chauveau, directed by Valerie Cogan, designed by Paul Minter.

Woman as UNMARRIED MOTHER – RUTH, *aged thirty-nine*
Woman as MOTHER WHO NEVER WAS – NAOMI, *aged seventy, Jewish*
Woman as FAILED MOTHER – MIRIAM, *aged forty-five*
Woman as MOTHER EARTH – DEBORAH, *aged thirty-five*

I imagine that for each character the actress will add or discard one or two garments, perhaps a wig, perhaps a small prop, to help. But the portrayals will depend mainly upon acting. It should not matter if the actress is and looks thirty-five when she is portraying a much older woman. The challenge in these vignettes is to convey an *impression* of the personalities, through timbre and pace of voice, and through physical gestures, such as the folding of clothes by Ruth.

The four settings are indicated by one or two pieces of furniture. All are visible on the stage. The actress moves into each for her different portrayal – except for the 'supermarket'; in this scene she can push her trolley round and round the stage reaching up and down into space, 'shopping' from shelves.

Aged thirty-nine.

A bed, two suitcases on it, a pile of clothes beside each, and a huge stuffed monkey.

She's packing for a holiday, and talking, in mock anger, to her child, unseen in another room.

(*Calling.*) And I'll tell you something else, Divine Brat, I may love and adore you but I'm not packing your case. I'm packing my own case but your'n will remain unpacked by anyone but *you*!

(*To herself.*) Does she imagine I've built up this business so's she can sit on her pretty little bum and complain of the world's cruelty? Well I haven't!

(*Calling.*) Do you imagine I've built up this business so's you can sit on your pretty little bum and complain of the world's cruelty! Well I haven't!

(*To herself.*) It's a hard world run by men who are frightened of women, and I'm going to make certain she's independent of them.

(*Calling.*) I want you to learn everything – from threading a needle to cooking a dinner, from running a career to packing a case! It's a hard world run by men who are frightened of women, and I'm going to make certain you're independent of them.

(*To herself.*) She's got me repeating myself. I'm going mad. She'll lose me to the asylum!

(*Calling.*) So you don't have a father! I'm a criminal! You've told me a thousand times. *I'm* tired of hearing it and *you* should be tired of telling it, now come and help me pack. It's our first skiing holiday and we have to think carefully about what we take or we'll freeze.

(*To herself.*) I'm tolerating no nonsense from her. Children! You never win! If I'd have married he'd've been the wrong father; if he'd been the right father I'd've been the wrong mother; if we'd both been right she'd've said our happiness was excluding her! Well if she thinks I'm going to encourage self-pity she's got another think coming!

Two sweaters, or four? For a change? Four! And you can be certain I'll leave behind the only one I care about.

(*Pause, listening.*) Yes, I know, fathers are important. But lesson number one: no one is indispensable. Lesson number two: face reality, don't succumb to it. And lesson number three: girls who cry miss planes. (*Pause.*) What do you mean the last one's a proverb. Are you trying to teach me the difference between a lesson and a proverb?

(*To herself.*) Bloody kids! They'll even stop crying to point out your mistakes. And I've got plenty and doesn't she know them and doesn't she tell me them.

(*Calling.*) And what's so special about men anyway? You think I can't teach you to ski? You think I can't make campfires? You think I can't giggle and horseplay in the snow?

(*To herself.*) She's right! I can't! I hate skiing, I hate snow, and I hate all that cold and those hearty, healthy, rosy-cheeked people. Especially healthy rosy-cheeked women. And what's more I hate being *alone* on holiday with her. But what can I do for God's sake! I didn't purchase a husband, *she* hasn't inherited a father, and that's that.

And then there's the question of what books to take, and games. Or do they have games there? I don't know. What do I know. What do I know about skiing resorts, except they're places where you break legs.

(*Calling.*) A father's expensive, anyway. He spends his money on possessions, he takes up most of the space, you end up revolving around his needs, and before you know it *you're* made to feel guilty for imprisoning *him*! Trust me, Divine Brat, we'll find a temporary father on the slopes. You'll fall, I'll weep, they'll come running!

(*To herself.*) Full of consolation, masculine protectiveness, and suppressed fantasies. God! I hate them! (*Pause.*) God! I need them. (*Pause.*) God! I hate myself for needing them! (*Pause.*) I must be crazy. A skiing holiday! The world slips under my feet every day, why should I wear skis to help it!

Foolish girl! Does she imagine I don't need a partner for myself as much as she needs a dad? (*Pause.*) Well, not *all* the time, but just now and then, when I'm on heat, or when she's hating me, hired! like cars by the hour, for a day or a week. I mean it wouldn't be so bad if we could hire them for just a year, and then take them back, like a library book you've finished reading. After all, no man is an *endless* book.

(*Calling.*) That's a proverb for you: no man is an endless book!

(*To herself.*) And I knew *that* from the start, as though God had singled me out for protection! Ruth, he warned me, no man is an endless book. (*Pause.*) Besides, I wanted to be dependent on *no* one. No one! (*Pause.*) That's an absurd thing to say. Live alone and you talk nonsense to yourself – no one to contradict you! No one is ever independent. If I needed no one else I'd need her. The Divine Brat!

(*Calling.*) Hey, Divine Brat! You made a list, there's an empty case waiting to be filled up, now come and do it. Please! If you don't pull yourself together you'll have to ski naked, and frozen pubic hairs are rough on the skin.

(*To herself.*) She didn't find it funny. I suppose if you haven't any pubic hairs it isn't very funny! But that's no reason not to laugh. I'm her mother. She's supposed to humour me. No sense of humour! My daughter has no sense of humour. Children are by nature morbid, give them something to be sad about and at once they're happy.

(*Calling.*) Hey! Did I ever tell you how the world knows Jesus was Jewish! One: he didn't leave home till he was thirty-five. Two: *he* thought *she* was a virgin. Three: *she* thought *he* was God! (*Pause.*) I made a joke! Your terrible mother made a joke! Laugh for God's sake. It may not happen again.

> *Waits. No response.*

What more can I do for you? I work for you, shop for you, plot for you, cook for you, I bleed for you, wash for you, long for you, fear for you, (*Sings it.*) I sing for you, knit for you, weep for you, ache for you, (*Picks up stuffed monkey and dances with it.*) and I dance, dance, dance, dance, daaaaaaaance for you!

> *Flops on bed.*

(*To herself.*) I'm a performing idiot! That's what mothers are, performing idiots!

(*Calling.*) Mothers are performing idiots!

(*To herself.*) What kind of respect can I expect? Wallop

her, that's what I should do. That's what a good father would do. She wants a father? Right! I'll show her what a father is. (*Wailing like a child.*) 'I want a daddy.' Wallop! 'I won't go to school.' Wallop! 'I don't want to go skiing.' Wallop! She doesn't want to be happy? Intelligent? Independent? Self-sufficient? Strong? Wallop! Wallop! Wallop, wallop, wallop!

(*Calling.*) Divine Brat! Come here and be walloped.

(*To herself.*) Wouldn't do any good. Last time I walloped her it was me who cried. (*Pause.*) But she's right. Times like these you need a man. Damn them! Damn them, damn them, damn them! (*Pause.*) Ignore her, that's what I'll do.

(*Calling.*) I'm ignoring you! (*One breath.*) I'm packing my cases and if you don't pack yours then there'll be the usual last-minute rush and you'll have to leave half of what you need behind because there won't be time to look for it because it'll all be buried in those corners of the flat you manage to find and I never knew existed and I'll get the blame because when it suits you I'm the older more responsible member of this family so COME THIS INSTANT WHEN I CALL YOU!

(*To herself. Complete change of mood.*) Besides, I grabbed my chance. Who would've wanted to marry me? Plain, graceless, difficult, clever. Impossible combination for a man to accept. Could hardly get one to talk to me let alone sleep with me! And to marry me? Never! So I saw this man and I said to myself – 'him!' Paid a fortune to be made up, used all my will power to be gracious and tried hard not to be clever. Result? The Divine Brat!

(*Calling.*) You, Divine Brat!

(*To herself.*) She'll think I've gone mad.

    Begins to pack daughter's case.

And it was worth every tear of it. Every humiliation, every lie, every struggle. *She* was what I wanted. Exactly. The way she looks, the way she thinks, the way she feels, the way she loves, quarrels, smiles, screams, sings, teases, dances, cries, blackmails, questions, observes, perseveres. Perseveres? Stubborn, more like. What am I doing? I'm packing her case. Look at me! I'm giving in to her again.

(*Calling.*) Divine Stubborn Brat! Come here! You may need your daddy but your mother needs you.

> *She opens her arms. Waits.*

(*To herself.*) But don't you ever take advantage of that, Divine Brat, not ever.

> *Smiles. The child is coming.*

> *Slow fade.*

NAOMI

Aged seventy.

Four features distinguish NAOMI*'s personality: a paperback book, which she has read so many times that all its pages are loose, but she continually reaches for it to read a sentence or two, as though needing to stay in touch with something familiar, loved; the song she hums every so often, a negro lullaby 'Oh ma babby, ma curly-headed babby' – an unconscious humming. Third, a constant appetite for 'news', about anything! Finally, her habit of sitting in her armchair with one leg cocked over an arm.*

She sits in a faded leather armchair leaning against a tatty, crocheted cover, made long ago by herself. She will sit in this armchair throughout.

A small, round table covered by a faded cloth is at her side. On it is the paperback book, a dusty telephone, an opened egg in its cup, some fingers of toast, a cup of tea, jug of milk, sugar bowl. At her side, on the floor, a pot of tea and tin of biscuits. On the television squats a dead pot-plant. The atmosphere is one of resignation and neglect.

As lights go up the television is on but sound is down. NAOMI *is fumbling with her broken paperback book; she has to turn a page and as all the leaves are loose she's having difficulty. It is our first image of her.*

She reads, eyes close to the page. Sighs. Replaces book. Sips from her cup of tea. Pauses to look outside of the cup, something stuck to it. She scratches it away. Yesterday's crumbs. Shrugs. Drinks again.

She faces television set. Hums, gazes. Then, realising there's no sound, she leans forward to turn it up louder. Sits.

And sits.

Phone rings. Seems not to hear it. Then does.

Hello?

Oh hello, Danny.

All right, thank you. Any news?

What?

I can't hear you, this is a terrible line. What did you say?

Wait a minute.

    She leans forward to turn down television.

Hello?

That's better.

She pours herself another cup of tea, reaches for biscuit tin which she places between her knees to facilitate pulling off the lid, takes out biscuits, replaces lid and box, dips biscuit into tea.

It has all been done with one hand, the other holds the phone; she's talking meanwhile.

I'm watching television.

No, there's never anything worthwhile. I just switch it on and think of other things. Any news?

What was that?

I can't hear you.

Yes, I've had my supper, thank you.

A boiled egg and toasted fingers with butter.

Because I can't be bothered to make anything more. Besides I had a good lunch.

Some meat and cheese and a banana.

It's enough. What more do I need!

What?

I can't hear you.

Yes, the flat's clean.

Yes, I've dusted.

No, I'll hoover tomorrow.

Tomorrow, tomorrow, I'll hoover tomorrow. Stop nagging. Any news?

I'm not shouting. Any news?

David is what?

No, my ears don't need syringing. I keep telling you, it's a bad line. David is what?

Leaving his job? What's he going to do?

What?

Travel! Where's he going to travel?

'Everywhere' is a big place. What's he going to use for money?

Well, he won't get far on that, will he?

You 'what' for him?

I can't hear, say it again.

Oh, this is a shocking line, shocking. You 'what' for him?

A.

B.

What?

E?

Oh, C. Yes, A – C –

H.

D?

What?

B?

Oh, E. A – C – H – E. You 'ache' for him. Well aching won't do much good, he's got to go through it himself, learn the hard way like we all did, only some of us didn't learn, and some of us who did – learned too late.

You want me to do what?

To speak to who?

You want me to speak to Abe Border? Who's Abe Border?

Oh, you want me to speak into a tape recorder. What for?

Don't be a silly boy, Danny. I can't remember all those years back. And anyway, who wants to? I miss nothing. It was all terrible. My childhood was terrible, my youth was terrible. I missed a married life, which I know some people would say was not so terrible but I'd like to have decided for myself, and here I am. No one in the middle of nowhere with no more chances. Nothing good to remember, nothing good to miss.

All right, you'll come when you come. I'm not going anywhere.

Yes, you too. Thank you for calling.

I promise, I promise, I'll hoover tomorrow.

> *Replaces phone. Sadly looks around. Runs her finger over top of television and wipes dust on her apron.*
>
> *The exchange has made her sad. She reaches out for the book. Fumbles and reads. Sighs. Replaces book. Returns to watching television without turning up the sound. Hums to herself. Then –*

'Tell me what you miss from those years, tell me what you remember from those years.' Silly boy! What can I remember? My memory's gone to sleep. I looked after an invalid mother, then I looked after a sick sister, and now there's no one to look after me – *that's* what I remember. A life gone! No sodding justice in this world.

> *Hums. Then –*

I suppose it could wake up, my memory, if Prince Charming came along.

The thought amuses her and she giggles. It is a special, innocent moment, full of old age charm.

Prince Charming.

Hums. Then —

I remember once, a Christmas time, it was when we were living in the East End, still young girls, and all the other children were talking about their Christmas stocking, and how it was going to be filled. Of course it was really pillow cases they hung up because you couldn't get much into a stocking, could you? So I thought, well, I'll also try it, see what happens. Jewish people don't celebrate Christmas but maybe Father Christmas couldn't tell the difference between Jews and Christians. I'd take a chance! So I hung up a huge pillow case and when I woke on Christmas morning I rushed to look and found — it was empty!

It's been like that ever since.

Phone rings.

Hello, Danny? Twice in one day? You've got a little news for me?

What?

You feel low? What are *you* low about?

About me? Don't worry about me, worry about yourself and your family, I'm all right. I just had a good laugh.

About Prince Charming. (*Giggles.*)

Explain! Explain! How can I explain? Tell me some news instead.

Well, what can you do. I'm an old woman who had no

childen, and that's what happens to old women who have no children: they grow old with no children. Now think of some news to tell me.

I'm watching a comedy show.

I know it's a terrible show but I put it on to hear a human voice.

Well, it's true, isn't it? You ring me and that's good of you but yours is the only voice I hear.

I'm not sad.

I'm *not* sad.

I'm not *sad*! I've just had the stuffing knocked out of me and that's that. Stop worrying, and think of some news to tell me. It'll soon be over, besides.

No, I'm not trying to depress you. I'm facing reality. How much longer do you think I've got?

What?

What?

Ten or fifteen years? Oh, Danny! Don't be wicked. You wish me ten or fifteen years more of *this*? Don't be wicked! I'm not wicked to you.

No, I've already told you. I've dusted today and I'll hoover tomorrow.

I promise.

Yes, tomorrow. I'll hoover tomorrow.

You're a good nephew.

I promise.

Tomorrow.

Bye.

Phone down.

She reaches for her book. Fumbles. Reads. Replaces it. Watches silent screen.

'Dust,' he tells me, 'and hoover! A little bit each day!' If I had someone to hoover for, I'd hoover! 'Do it for yourself,' he says. 'It'll raise your spirits!' Spirits! It's enough I get up in the mornings. 'Remember, you're a senior citizen,' he says. Humbug! I'm not a senior citizen, I'm a very dried-up tired old woman. 'Are you a middle-aged citizen?' I ask him. 'Do you call your children junior citizens? Young is young, and old is old,' I tell him. 'Don't insult me!'

She leans forward to the flickering screen, runs a finger over a part of it. Then rubs the same spot. And again, more vigorously. Finally, she takes her hand-kerchief, spits on it, and cleans the entire screen.

When she's finished she looks at it in amazement; it shines brightly back at her.

Now that really *was* dirt.

She looks slowly around the room as though realising for the first time how she has allowed it all to go to pieces.

She reaches for the dead pot-plant, gazes at it sadly, a symbol of self-neglect. Replaces it. Settles back in the armchair, one leg cocked over the arm. Hums. Stops. Shivers, a sudden chill runs through her. She hugs herself. Hums. Stops.

What I really miss is to be held. No one's held me for years. Not for years and years. Imagine!

Hums. Stops.

Wish he'd have been my son.

Pause.

Hums.

Lights slowly fade.

MIRIAM

Aged forty-five.

Smartly dressed. She's talking to a psychiatrist.

It begins with a scream. But it's not mine. I was just born with it. Like a pea in an empty tin can, it rattles when I try to move. No! The wrong image. Like a tumour, growing as I grow. No! Not that, either. It doesn't grow, it diminishes. And it's not in me. I am it, someone else's scream, but diminished, like an echo. (*Pause.*) Who knows?

My mother was unworldly.

Do you know what it's costing me to sit before you and say all this? Do you know with what confidence and happiness and expectation I entered marriage and motherhood? The plans I had, the theories I'd read, the careful thought that went into those girls? I couldn't wait to have chilen. Do you know that?

Some women want happy husbands as their monu-ment, some fight for careers, or plan wealth, or scheme for status. But not me. My monument was to be my children. (*Pause.*) Who knows?

My mother was unworldly.

You think that was the cause for the mess, don't you? I wanted it for *my* sake and not theirs. It looks like that doesn't it? But it's not true. Not if you look at what actually happened: I didn't have special ambitions for them. It wasn't that I wanted one to be a doctor, another to be a film star, another to run a business. Of course that would have been lovely – security, glory, a sense of achievement. And why not? But no. Instead I said 'I don't care what you do as long as you're happy'!

'Happy'! 'I don't care what you do'! Sentimental nonsense! I cared all right, but I pretended I didn't. What I should have done is pushed them, urged, nagged, scolded. But no, I thought, if I show too much concern they'll react against my nagging.

And who knows, perhaps they would have done. Some children have natures so perverse they'll only act by opposites. (*Pause.*) Who knows?

My mother was unworldly.

On the other hand some mothers can never do right. No matter what they do they strike the wrong note. Perhaps *that's* what was wrong. My style. All people have style don't they. When you say about somebody 'Oh, *they* can get away with murder' you mean they can do the wrong thing and it works, while some of us, even when we do the right thing, do it badly. Perhaps that was me: the wrong person to be right. Some of us are like that. We're just the wrong people to be right. God knows!

My style? (*Pause.*) Style, style, style! (*Pause.*) Echoes. Diminished echoes.

My mother was unworldly.

Do you realise how humiliating I find it to talk to a psychoanalyst?

The ultimate defeat! Well, how else can it be interpreted? Your friends have no resources, your family have no resources, and you have no resources. All known human sympathy and comprehension sucked dry. So – the shrink! The last resort before whom you must confess, wail, weep, reveal, betray.

No, I'm not going to betray my husband. It's tempting to blame him but I won't. We were together in all this. I don't mean we agreed, I mean we *shared* the responsibility. In fact we *didn't* agree. He wanted to shout and slap them when they misbehaved. I wouldn't let him. Can't bear coarseness, or violence, or shouting. Talk! Reason! Explain!

I was wrong, wasn't I? Not all misbehaviour is explicable.

Yes it is! Pleasure! Misbehaviour provides pleasure. (*Thinks about this.*) Can such pleasures be talked, reasoned, explained away? Thwart it and you have violence, don't you? (*Pause.*) Who knows?

My mother was unworldly.

But it was unacceptable pleasure and I failed to let them know it was unacceptable. Sometimes you should shout. Show your anger, your outrage. Outrage is important. I lost my capacity for outrage, *that* was the problem. I confused outrage for moral righteousness. (*Pause.*) Though I never did know what was wrong with a little moral righteousness. I was made to feel ashamed to express it, but – I don't know, they knew I loved them enough, I could have afforded an occasional slap. But there! It was not in me. I couldn't. Could I help my nature?

My nature? (*Pause.*) My nature, nature, nature! (*Pause.*) Echoes. Diminished echoes. (*Pause. Angrily.*) Unworldly! That's what I was, unworldly! I didn't understand the world, couldn't piece it together. And I still don't, and I still can't!

Why? Why? Why? Damn it, why? Others could. Others made perfect sense of it, but not me. Not *me*!

Pause.

My mother was unworldly.

Pause.

But I prevented my husband from showing his anger, and that was wrong, wasn't it? It's good to be different, providing you give people space for it.

Space! The secret to all relationships, isn't it? Husband and wife, friend and friend, state and individual, parent and child – space! Each must be allowed their proper space.

So they were badly brought up, my poor daughters. Yanked up through life by one arm instead of two, because I didn't allow their father to be what he is. I didn't give him his space.

Not true! He didn't allow their mother to be what *she* is! He didn't give me *my* space.

Why didn't he? Why didn't I?

Why? Why? (*Pause.*) Who knows?

My mother was unworldly.

I'm not even the original scream. My whole life is just an echo of someone else's echo whose life was an echo of someone else's echo, whose life was an echo of an echo of an echo of an echo of an echo of an echo . . .

But who was the scream?

My poor girls. Echoes! Thin echoes! And each echo becomes thinner.

Pause.

She utters a loud scream. It seems not to come from her.

Blackout.

DEBORAH

Aged thirty-five.

She wheels a supermarket trolley around, reaching up for this, down for that, and talking to 'another housewife' at her side.

She's energetic, defiant, full of delight in her life.

Electronic sound of cash register constantly in background.

Me a prisoner? Never! Those poor men, tied to their jobs, tied to their hours, caught in a rush to a top they'll never reach in a thousand years – they're the prisoners, they're the slaves! But not me! I enjoy the freedom of my home too much.

Look out for the date on that yoghurt. (*Calls to assistant.*) Young man! Take this batch away. They're two days old. (*To neighbour.*) Mustn't let them get away with anything.

Yes, I have three of them, and if it wasn't so tiring and costly and boring to be married to a woman who was always fat and pregnant I'd have a dozen of them! Love them! Everything about them. I loved carrying them, giving birth to them, suckling them. I loved changing their smelly nappies, washing their smelly bums with smelly oils, powdering their fat bodies with smelly powders – all of it! Every smelly second of it! It's what I always wanted to do, what I still want to do, and what I'm supremely equipped to do. So just let anyone dare bully me into thinking it's me who's the prisoner.

Don't buy that! Frozen pastry! Doesn't work. Makes your pies taste like leather. I made a meat pie from it last week and it felt as though we were eating minced meat in an old boot. Make your own. Better! Get the feel of that flour and butter in your hands. Lovely! Like kneading a man's bum. Lovely!

I mean I'd *always* wanted to marry, always wanted to have children, always wanted two boys and one girl and that's what I got! Born lucky! Everything fell into place. Just as I'd dreamed.

Oh, look! This week's special offer. Candles! I'm mad about candles. I burn them all the time. From the moment I get up I light a candle so's to have a moving flame in front of me. Some people hate them. Remind them of death. Not me! 'Someone's at home!' it says. 'A person's around, waiting, preparing, looking out for you!' If I had my way I'd live by candlelight, and heat by firelight.

Now *that's* a good buy. Three packets of meat for the price of two. You can stock up for a couple of weeks with that. Why don't you take some pork, steak, and lamb – one of them's free!

No escaping the fact – I'm a shopper! I love shopping. I don't mean I'm the sort to go a mile to save a penny but I love abundance. And don't get me wrong when I say that. My children are not spoilt or over-fed. They know about poverty, they know about hard work, and they know everything has to be earned. *And* all the dictionaries and encyclopedias are there on the shelves to help them. Science and music, rivers and religions, phrases and fables, etymology, mythology, anthropology – everything! Everything's on offer in our house. They can reach to any shelf and learn about where they come from. There's even a dictionary of chivalry, because I want them polite, grateful and conscious of the difficult world they live in – but! Oh! The pleasure I get seeing them eat a good meal, the reward to see them feel confident. I don't want them smug but I do want them courageous. And generous. I can't bear meanness of any sort. Abundance! Spiritually, intellectually, emotionally. I love abundance.

Now there's something you ought to try. It's not cheap but it's a real delicacy. Something to surprise them with. Made in Denmark. An absolutely scrumptious biscuit. Melts in your mouth.

Sorry! But what can I do? I enjoy feeding people. In fact I've often thought that I'd hire myself out for a fee as a shopper. There are some people, you know, who hate shopping. Simply hate it. Not me. I bet I could earn quite a living doing other people's shopping. Fancy! Being paid to do something you like. How I'd love to spend other people's money shopping up all the things I couldn't afford myself. That would really be exciting, like living other people's lives. Paid to be everybody's mother. Ha!

Now if you'll listen to me you'll take those soaps on cheap offer. I saw them fifty pence more in the chemist yesterday. French soaps. Lovely!

I get very angry when people ask what I do and I tell them and they say 'Oh, you don't have a profession then?' I *do* have a profession. A very skilful profession. A profession full of different skills. Not only cooking, washing, ironing, but organising. People don't realise the organisation that goes into running a household. Budgeting, stocking up, planning ahead. And the imagination that's required! All those details that make my home a haven, a womb, an anchor, a magnet! I don't want them to take me for granted but I do want them to be certain of me. That gives me a great satisfaction that does, to be relied upon. I'm there! I'm willing! I begrudge no effort! And the result is I've made a place no one ever wants to leave. A treasure house full of little goodies in cupboards, snacks in fridge, crisp sheets on the bed once a week, different soaps, copper shining on the walls, shelves and leather dusted and smelling of pine, always a clean shirt, a fresh hot towel, a home-cooked meal. And to remind them of nature the house is covered with pot-plants creeping and crawling all over the place which I water and prune and talk to.

And if my husband wasn't allergic to animal smells I'd have lots of animals roaming around like lion cubs and koala bears. I'm needed, wanted, depended upon. I glory in it, bathe in it, thrive on it!

Me the prisoner? Never!

Blackout.

Yardsale

A play in eight scenes

Yardsale was first broadcast by BBC Radio 3 on 6 October 1984 with Sheila Steafel, produced by Margaret Windham. It had its stage premiere on 12 August 1985 at the Edinburgh Festival with Jeannie Fisher, directed by Eric Standige. Its first London performance was in a double-bill with *Whatever Happened to Betty Lemon?* on 17 February 1987 at the Lyric Theatre Studio, Hammersmith, with Brenda Bruce, directed by the author and designed by Jackie Pilfold.

SCENE ONE – THE HOMECOMING

Brooklyn, New York State. A suburban house. Front door closing.

STEPHANIE, *a primary school teacher, forty-eight years old, returns home, takes off her coat, boots, scarf . . . prepares a meal. All is mimed.*

The ticking of a clock divides the parts.

I'm late, I'm late, don't tell me – I'm late! But there are reasons. *Not* because I kept any of my children behind in class. *Not* because I was kept talking by one of those drive-you-crazy-my-child's-genius-is-being-neglected mothers. *Not* because the bus was held up by all this snow which made my boots wet and reminds me I've got to buy a new pair which it so happens I saw on sale in that store which seems to have a non-stop-all-the-year-round sale so you wonder where they got their stock from. Not because of any *one* of those things but because *all* of them put together plus I saw this gorgeous pullover for you which I *had* to buy and they didn't have your size but they told me they could get it sent over from another of their stores which wouldn't take a minute they said but it took thirty so I'm five minutes later than usual but here it is and here I am, your one-and-only Stephanie and soon we can eat. (*Sung as in 'Jeal-ous-y'.*) Steph-an-ie!

Sheldon? Don't *you* delay now. We promised we'd go hear Lord What's-His-Name from England lecture on who has stolen what art treasures from whom and should they be returned. So move your butt and join me in the kitchen for a rousing chorus of 'Summertime', and we'll chop mushrooms together. Remember:

Procrastination is the thief of time:
Year after year it steals till all are fled
And to the mercies of a moment leaves
The vast concerns of an eternal scene.

Lord What's-His-Name may not be a vast concern but let's not leave ourselves to the mercies of a moment.

Sheldon? Sheldon? Only *five* minutes late. Is he upstairs in the bathroom and I uttered all that to the air?

Looks high and low.

Sheldon? Are you *sulking* somewhere because I'm five minutes late? You can't call 'five minutes' late! Sheldon, are you *any*where in the house? (*Beat.*) Has he kept some of *his* kids behind in class?

Begins to prepare meal.

Mimes slicing, slapping, and frying.

Poor Sheldon. It's harder work teaching teenagers than primary school kids. I'm luckier than him. Wrong! Than 'he is'.

From five years old to seven you're embarrassed, from seven to nine you're grateful, from nine to eleven you're beginning to be confident, after that everything collapses and you've got to start all over again: confidence-building, ego-tripping, sexual-flaunting, parent-confronting, teacher-challenging, world-mocking, everything boiling and troubling and nuclear exploding. Right, Sheldon? Right, Stephanie!

Sheldon, are you sure you're not somewhere in the house? I know your tricks, you let me talk to myself and that way imagine you're hearing what I really think but never tell you. I'm not one of your devious-imagining-they're-subtle women, you know, or one of your hesitant-imagining-they're-thoughtful women, or one of your obscure-imagining-they're-profound women. I tell you *every*thing and say what I mean which is not always sensible, you're right, but there you are, I am *who* I am, *what* I am, *that* I am so you can listen to me talking to myself all the time and you won't find out more than you already know about me. Sheldon?

I've always been luckier than him. Than 'he is'. To begin with I've got him and he's only got me. (*Beat.*) Now then, Stephie, don't let your feminist friends hear you talk that way, putting yourself down. (*Singing.*) Steph-an-ie! So what if your breasts droop and you've got piles? Teachers sit down they get piles! Poets and long-distance truck drivers also get piles. And if Sheldon had had three children his breasts would also droop. (*Beat.*) More than they do! (*Laughs.*) Naughty. You should be naughty more often. Right, Sheldon? Right, Stephanie. (*Singing.*) Steph-an-ie!

There! That's the steaks slapped and peppered, the potatoes scrubbed and baking, the mushrooms chopped and frying, the tomatoes grilling, (*Singing.*)

> . . . an' the livin' is easy.
> Fish are jumpin and the cotton is high.
> Oh your daddy's rich and your ma is good
>   lookin'.
> Hush, little baby don't you cry.

(*Beat.*) I wish I *did* have a baby. Even who cried. Just one more time. All over again. (*Beat.*) The house is so empty with the children gone. (*Beat.*)

Think I'll put on some music, perhaps a candle, freshen my make-up a little, drooping breasts or no drooping breasts. (*Singing.*) Steph-an-ie!

> *She dims lights. Lights a candle. Presses a cassette*

*player – second movement of Barber Violin Concerto –
and moves into the bedroom.*

SCENE TWO – THE DISCOVERY

STEPHANIE *clutches a letter.*

Oh no, Sheldon. Not me. Please not to me. Please,
please not to this old friend. Not after twenty-five years
and three children and all that history, Sheldon.
Twenty-five years and three children *is* history: rich and
private and all ours. Ours! Ours and yours and mine
and theirs and all rich and private and not for sharing.
With anyone. No one. Oh please God don't let it be
happening to me. Please, oh please.

She weeps.

Slowly controls herself.

(*Reading.*) 'My dear Stephie.' *My* dear Stephie? His?
He's leaving and claiming me at the same time. Strange
man. 'My dear Stephie. I must go. We care about one
another but there is no more we have to give one
another. Not you to me, not me to you. We say nothing
at meal times, we feel nothing at bedtimes, we know
everything and too much and nothing is a surprise.
Curiosity gone, nerve-ends dead, mechanical. We are
boring. I need to be able to surprise someone.'

I'm surprised, Sheldon, am I surprised! Don't go, look!
I'm *very* surprised. (*Beat.*) I'm mortified. (*Beat.*) I'm
destroyed.

Music fades. Lights dim.

SCENE THREE — THE DEPRESSION
She is curled up in bed. Foetal position.

I will lie here in this bed and never get up. They can do without me in school. The children don't need me. For weeks I've done nothing but yell at them, anyway. I will lie here in this bed and invent agonies for her.

What did I do wrong?

Husband-thief!

I will lie here in this bed and invent agonies fit for a husband-thief.

(*Shouting.*) Thief! Thief! Husband-thief!

Was my skin clammy? Was my voice droning? Were my thoughts boring?

I would like to pull out her nails. No. Better. I would like to tie her up to watch while I pull out *his* nails. Better. I would like to tie them both up while I mark her and castrate him and *then* pull out their nails. First one from him then one from her then one from him then one from her. She loves him, she loves him not, she loves him, she loves him not, she loves him. (*Beat.*) She loves him. (*Beat.*) Oh Christ does she love him?

What, what did I do wrong?

I will lie here in this bed and drown. Who needs a teacher with such violence in her? (*Beat.*) They say you're whole life flashes by you when you drown. I'm drowning and I want my whole life to flash by *me* to see where *I* went wrong.

Stephanie! Why should you think *you* went wrong? (*Singing.*) Steph-an-ie!

I would like to see her run over by a car. I would like to see her struck blind. I would like to take shit and throw it on her. I will lie here in this bed and imagine these things.

Did my breath smell? Did I talk nonsense? Did I lack style?

I've been a good woman, Sheldon. Faithful, patient, a companion, a friend, and I laid on my back more times than I cared to for you, you know that? There! More times than I cared to. Surprises? You want surprises? *There's* a surprise for you. I opened my legs and thought about cooking the next day's meal while you heaved and puffed and made all those absurd shrieks you informed me was passion. 'Passion!' you yelled at me. 'Be passionate! Moan!' I'm moaning, Sheldon. Listen how I'm moaning now. Oh, God! How I moan. I will lie here in this bed and never get up and I will moan the rest of my days.

Was I too loud, too intense, too dry? Did something in me stop long ago?

You don't know what you've done. You can't know or you wouldn't have done it. Did you think? You *never* think. A woman past her best, her three children grown up, disappeared into their own lives. I've invested in you my youth, my womanhood, the secrets of my body, my fund of love, friendship, wisdom and patience, and my investments should be showing a return, damn it! I should be plucking the profits by now!

But you have taken them. Run off with them. Snatched them from under my nose to share with someone else. Thief, Sheldon! Miserable bastard thief! Criminal thief! Stop, thief! Stop, stop, thief! Stop, murderer!

I will lie here in my bed and never get up and be in darkness, and I will moan and see no one. Ever again.

SCENE FOUR – THE PHONE CALL

Maxie? Maxie, have you got a second? Well not a second, a couple of days, actually. Yes, I received the carrot cake and the chicken breasts and the saucepan full of chilli con carne – thank you but you're cooking for armies I'm a single woman, remember? Nevertheless, I thank you, thank you, all of you. You worry, you nag, but now – don't interrupt me. I've got to talk.

I've been thinking. Thinking and remembering and remembering and thinking and I've made discoveries and come to conclusions. I'm a fool! Worse, I'm a dishonest fool! I'm a fool because I married a man I never really loved, and I'm dishonest because I *pretended* I loved him.

I *never* loved him. I didn't even like him. I *thought* I loved him because he said he loved *me* and – and this is the trap into which, oh boy! didn't I fall: he was the first man ever to say it. '*I love you.*' Imagine! I was twenty-four and beginning to think I was a leper or my breath was permanently putrefied, and along comes this man, this young god built on fresh eggs, orange juice, his mother's chopped liver, and the playing fields of Brooklyn High, with green eyes and curly hair and a cherubic smile from Botticelli which you want to eat, and says '*I love you!*' To me! Who could resist? He had to be an extraordinary human being to love me, and who was I not to be in love with an extraordinary human being!

But think about him. I mean when I think about him, I mean – oh good God and little fishes – did he have a mind? I mean – a *mind*? You know what I mean by a mind don't you? That lovely thing that takes from here and connects with there and interprets this and illuminates that. Him? Ponderous like a hedgehog. Not one

prick but many! Every day he was run over by a world
he never comprehended.

And what conversation! He floated the debris of *other*
people's battles. His thoughts used to go on for so long
his words would forget where they began. Dialogue like
driftwood, sodden and cut off. He was a thief! What
could you expect? He stole my youth and other
people's arguments. A thief!

And was he witty? Was he ever! *She* was witty. I've got
to give the husband-thief that. Smart, witty, rich and
healthy. So healthy it made you sick to look at her, you
know the type I mean? But him? Jokes fell off him like
shoes fall off tired old men. He told stories back to front
at the wrong time to the wrong people and for the
wrong reasons. He should never have tried to amuse.
It's a talent. He didn't have the talent. I used to get
embarrassed the way friends laughed from embarrass-
ment. But could *he* see it? Never! I never knew a man so
insensitive to what was happening around him. And his
puns? Did you ever know a grown person so relentlessly
persist in what must be one of the most boring literary
exercises ever conceived? It was an illness with him. A
mental twitch. Couldn't control himself. Some men
can't control their gas, he couldn't control his urge to
pun. And how he preened himself when he'd let it out.
Did you notice? That slow grin and that self-satisfied
glance around the company for approval? In one man
there resided (*Giggles.*) the farter, the pun and the holy
boast! Jokes! What am I making jokes for? I want to
make murder!

And you should have seen him in bed. Or rather you
shouldn't have seen him in bed. I'm sorry I ever saw
him in bed.
'Tonight's the night,' he'd announce. Subtly.
'Faw what, honey?' I used to put on a shy, southern

drawl and pretend I didn't know what he was on about. 'What night's this, sugar plum? You all surely don't mean – oh my, Sheldon, there's no stopping you I do declare.' And then he'd leap onto the bed in his altogether and start jumping up and down so's his shlong and spheroids flip-flapped about his thighs and I'd have to join him and bounce alongside of him so's my titties went flip-flap too and we made such a right old slap-smacking sound that I'm certain all the neighbours could hear. Sensuality, Maxie? He had the sensuality of a rhino stuck in mud, of a crocodile with false teeth, of a baboon full of fleas, a crab, a snail, a hyena, a pterodactyl! And all because he said he loved me.

What am I gonna do? What am I gonna do, what? Tell me, what? What, what, what?

Visits to help forget

SCENE FIVE – TO THE ART GALLERY

The Whitney Museum of American Art.

Go out, said my friends, visit places, out and about. Behave like the still-living, the still-curious, the still-mentally-alert-and-lively Stephanie we all knew and loved. (*Singing.*) Steph-an-ie! So! I'm out and about! But what am I out about? I'm out but what am I about? I should about turn and get out of this gallery that's what I should do, not stay here and look at this painter, Hopper, who I once loved because – I used to explain to our circle with earnest admiration – he exemplified the desperation and loneliness of men and women in a big city. Desperation! Loneliness! What am I looking at such paintings for? I'm not lonely and desperate enough? Go out, said my friends, visit places. But every place I go reminds me of him, of us, of our young years together. Stolen from me. Poisoned for me. Art galleries, museums, theatres, parks, bookshops, restaurants . . .

SCENE SIX – TO THE RESTAURANT

Serendipity – a restaurant famous in New York for its huge desserts.

. . . restaurants, take-aways, bars, flea-markets, even here – Serendipity's, where we'd each order an oversized knickerbocker glory or hot fudge sundae, and laugh and laugh and laugh. Poisoned!

What am I doing here? Mad-brained Stephanie! Don't you know that everywhere will be a sentimental journey? Everything will make you want to cry? I can't listen to music any more, I can't read poetry any more. I look at children, I cry. If it rains, I cry. The sun shines, I still cry. Massacres! Famine! Lovers holding hands! Cry, cry, cry! I've become a weepy.

Go out, said my friends, stay living. So I'm out and living and among crowds and I've never felt so lonely in all my life.

And do I need such a large dessert? Did I *ever* need such a large dessert? For such large desserts I've got my just desserts: fat and abandoned and growing fatter by the hour. This ice ceam it's like my marriage was – too big, too cold, and melting.

I hope he melts for her too, her the husband-thief. Smart, witty, rich, and ridiculously healthy – but a husband-thief no matter which way you look at it, and I'm looking at it all ways, all the time non-stop, scrutinising every detail of him, of me, of the past, to see what went wrong.

Go out, said my friends. Go jogging, go swimming, change your hairstyle, buy clothes, sell your house, get yourself massaged . . .

SCENE SEVEN – TO THE BOOKSHOP

Barnes and Noble.

A bookshop! What am I doing in a bookshop! I've got wall-to-wall books I haven't read, that I can't read, that I've no appetite to read, and here I am contemplating buying more when what I have didn't help. What would I do with more knowledge?

Stupid question! And you a teacher. You're full of stupid questions. Your brain's going to pieces. You're a joy to no one.

Anthologies of Shakespeare, anthologies of poetry. Reprints, art prints, paintings and sculptures, cartoons and cookery, books of photographs – of foreign places. Visit foreign places said my friends. Look at them! Who conceived so many editions! Who were they aimed at? Who's going to buy them for Christ's sake?

There's something about abundance makes you feel a theft here and there wouldn't be missed. (*Beat.*) What am I saying? Me! A remainder among remainders.

SCENE EIGHT – YARDSALE

Sunday morning church bells.

STEPHANIE *has just arrived. The first one there. No owner*

around. She waits outside the yard.

Go out, said my friends. Great! What does the notice say (*Reading.*) 'Yardsale-of-the-century takes place here. Sunday 18 September 1983. 9.30 sharp!' It *is* Sunday September 18 1983, and it's 9.45 – *sharp*!

Sharp? Why should time be sharp? 'On the dot' I understand. But sharp? On the sharp dot, maybe. Ah! Of course! Be here on the sharp dot of 9.30. Only they dropped 'dot'. (*Beat.*) And it's no longer 9.30. It's (*Looking at watch.*) 9.46 and 45 seconds. (*Pause.*) 9.46 and 50 seconds. (*Pause.*) 9.46 and 55 seconds. (*Pause.*) 9.47 – sharp!

Why do I talk about time all the time? And why am I *on* time all the time? Was I too pedantic? Too predictable? Is that what was wrong?

> *She enters the yard, talks as she picks up and regards objects.*

And why do I come nosing around sales looking, looking, as though I was a newly-wed with a new home to set up, always the first one here, even before the owner of the yard where the yardsale-of-the-century is about to take place is up? (*Pause.*) 9.48!

And that's how life goes and still no one's here to say hello, how are you, welcome to our yardsale-of-the-century, here's a tired old coat-hanger, a three-legged chair, an old-fashioned mirror, an old-fashioned type-writer, an old-fashioned waltz.

> *She hums waltz and waltzes a little. Stops. Pauses.*

9.49! (*Calling.*) Hey, mister, I could steal things. (*Beat.*) Trusting souls!

And what do we have here? A photo album. What kind of people throw away their relatives? In fact, come to think of it, what kind of people throw away their homes? You come to a sale like this and the question must be asked: why is all this discarded? Why should *I* want what someone *else* has discarded? What makes me think *I* could grow to love what someone else has squeezed all the love from? You come to a sale like this, the question has got to be asked.

Why do I ask? I know. You get tired of things. Even lovely things. I know. I had a husband got tired of me. In fact the person I knew was best at these yardsales-of-the-century, who knew which ones to come to and which to avoid, and where to look first, and what was a real bargain, and who was there sharp on the dot, on the sharp dot, on the dot – sharp! was the woman who talked my husband into thinking he was tired of me. But we won't talk about her. Even though she's smart, witty, rich and healthy we will not talk about her.

And what do we have here? A box full of postcards? I don't understand it. People write to you – it means something! A hello-how-are-you! Me, I hang on to 'hellos'. When your husband's gone after twenty-five years, three children, drooping breasts, dreams of murder, loss of faith, loss of confidence, loss of friends, a hysterectomy, and a year of piles – you need all the 'hellos' you can get. Miss Husband-Thief!

I know, I know. People *collect* cards: sea-views, mountains, old towns, old beauties, old stamps, old hellos.

Miss Husband-Thief. Miss Long Beak, Miss Hawk's Eyes, Miss Sensitive Schnozzle. From yardsales like this she furnished *his* new home. *Their* new home. 'Look at this!' she'd say, 'gold! and guess what I paid for it – two dollars!' Everything only ever cost her two dollars. And I'd get excited. Can you imagine? She was planning my husband's new home and I was getting excited. There's a fool for you. Would you believe a woman, who should know better because she is a woman, could be such a trusting fool? But we won't talk about her even though she's smart, witty, rich and healthy so it makes you sick.

It's a funny thing, a yardsale. You come to buy the things you didn't know you needed: baby carriage, cradle, trunks, cushions, curtains, shoes, candlesticks, ornaments, tools, linen, cardboard boxes full of – of – everything!

Why are they getting rid of all these items? Has someone died? The children gone? Why aren't the children inheriting? Didn't they *ever* love these things?

On the other hand – it can be exciting. A box full of everything is exciting. You got to admit, in a box full of little everythings you can find anything: beads, dolls, bricks, old thimbles, paperweights, pens – people actually collect old fountain pens. *I* never knew. *She* told me. Miss Useless Information.

She'd come back with these things and talk about them, where she was going to put them, how she was going to repair them, all about their period. She was clever. You've got to hand it to her, she knew things. I used to think how fortunate we were to have such a scintillating friend. 'Bright Eyes', I called her. I used to be proud we knew her. Boasted to our friends.

'You must meet our Miss Bright Eyes.' Miss Bright Eyes, Miss Knowledgeable, Miss Widely Read, Miss Much Travelled, Miss Stunning Taste, Miss Body Beautiful, Miss Goddamned Healthy Slimy Husband-Thief! I want to skin her alive and make her watch while I have handbags, gloves, and slippers-to-walk-on high fashioned from her slimy skin!

But we will not talk about her.

The old pens I've thrown out! And the baby carriages, cradles, trunks, cushions, curtains – husbands!

9.55!

What am I doing here? Pouncing on other people's used objects. I need new objects to have *new* memories, *my* memories. What do I need other people's old loves for? Mrs Garbage Items!

(*Calling.*) Hey, mister! Come already! A half hour I've been here. (*Weeping.*) *I* could steal things.

Fade.

Whatever Happened to Betty Lemon?

Whatever Happened to Betty Lemon? was first performed on 12 November 1986 at the Théâtre du Rond-Point, Paris, with Judit Magre, directed by Jean-Michel Ribes. Its first London performance was in a double-bill with *Yardsale* on 17 February 1987 at the Lyric Theatre Studio, Hammersmith, with Brenda Bruce, directed by the author and designed by Jackie Pilfold.

An Edwardian mansion flat.

Four areas in four corners: the front door, the study, the lounge, the kitchen. In the centre sits an electric wheelchair.

Off centre hangs a rope looking like a noose, but without the hangman's knot.

A whirring clock strikes seven. A lavatory flushes.

BETTY LEMON *appears, an old woman crippled by every-thing old age brings. Eccentric.*

She hobbles in with the aid of a walking frame. Surveys her flat. Another day is beginning. Gloom.

She looks at the noose – her daily companion with whom she converses. From it she draws strength, determination, as though she has deliberately erected a confrontation with the ultimate in order to be challenged.

A glance at the noose gives her resolve to face the day's battles with obstacles she's determined to overcome.

First to the front door to draw out a newspaper. A letter drops with it. She cannot be bothered to bend and pick it up. Now to the study to deposit the paper and collect a dirty cup and saucer. She cannot negotiate the frame and *the crockery. Abandons frame, reaches for a walking stick, hobbles to kitchen, deposits cup and saucer.*

Next – the lounge. Switch on TV. She cannot bear the early-morning cheerfulness. Turns it off. Hobbles to the front door to retrieve letter.

It has all been too exhausting. She struggles to the wheelchair into which she collapses.

BETTY. I didn't fucking plan it this way.

She extracts a letter from envelope.

(*Reading.*) 'Dear Lady Lemon . . .'

(*Savouring it.*) Lady Lemon. He promised he'd become a knight before he died. And he did. Then he died. Honoured and penniless. Though he spent his seed more than his pennies. Philandering bastard! Sir James Lemon! Socialist MP for Birmingham North. Knighted for services rendered to the nation. (*Beat.*) For services rendered at night to the fucking nation, more like!

(*Reading.*) 'Dear Lady Lemon . . .'

They call me Madam when I attend functions. 'Ma'am' sometimes. 'Honoured ma'am . . .' 'This plaque is dedicated, ma'am . . .' 'We would like you to meet, ma'am . . .' Me. Betty Lemon née Rivkind from Dalston Junction. If only they'd known my father. 'Rubbish!' he said, 'they all talk rubbish!'

(*Reading.*) 'Dear Lady Lemon . . .'

Madam Betty Lemon. Madam Betty Bitter Lemon. Madam Letty Batty Melon. Madam Batty Smelly Salmon. Smelly Betty Satin Button. Keep your hat on. Steel your baton. Bolt your belly-button, Betty. Oh belt up, Lady Lemon. (*Beat.*) You go daft when no one's around.

(*Reading.*) 'Dear Lady Lemon . . .'

You need someone around to stop you going daft. (*Beat.*) You wouldn't think I'd once been brainy. 'Watch out for brainy Betty Lemon,' they'd say. I was what they called – an intellectual.

(*To the noose.*) Difficult to be an intellectual when no one's around to challenge you.

(*Reading.*) 'Dear Lady Lemon. It is with great pleasure

that I inform you you have been chosen Handicapped
Woman Of The Year . . .'

*Incredulity. A thought so bizarre she can hardly
accommodate it.*

Handi-*what* of the year? Me? They telling me there's no
one more handicapped in the entire fucking universe
than me? And they're crowning me for it?

What glorious son of man conceived such blushing
laurels, such awesome accolades, such canonisation?

Thinks about it.

Champion Cripple three cheers! Happy Hobbler Of
The Year hurrah! The Season's Paraplegic Princess,
pah pom!

She's amused herself. Giggles. Stops abruptly.

(*Reading.*) 'As you may know, the Society For The
Elderly Handicapped holds an annual dinner at which
the Handicapped Woman Of The Year and the Handicapped Man Of The Year each address us for half an
hour on how they overcame their handicaps . . .'

Who says I over-fucking-came them?

She rehearses an address she will never deliver. (Not
to the audience.)

'My Lords, Ladies and Gentlemen, sound or unsound,
firm or infirm, those glowing with health or those ugly
with pain. I had an uncle – yes, even old women may
once have had uncles – I had an uncle who, recovering
from his third heart operation declared to me: "*You*
think the world is divided into *social* classes don't you?
As a socialist," he said, "*you* think the big divide in life
is between those who have and those who have not.
Well let me tell you you are wrong," he said. "The

world is divided into those who have health and those who do not have health. *That's* the only division that counts."

'Was he right or was he wrong, my Lords, Ladies and Gentlemen? (*Waits.*) Come on, let's hear from you. Was he right or was he bloody wrong? (*Waits. Miserably.*) Right! He was bloody right!'

Returns to letter.

(*Reading.*) 'We can offer you a fee . . .'

How very kind.

Now then, Betty Lemon. No bitterness. Remember you're a laie-dy, and though your famous, revered, socially responsible, ever-smiling, much-loved husband who talked rubbish all his life is dead they've not forgotten his wife, the loud-mouthed cow, the sardonic shadow, the caustic, unappreciative bitch at his side. Handicapped Woman Of The Year! Handi-Fucking-Capped-Woman-Of-The-Year-Betty-Lemon-honoured-and-remembered! You should feel proud. Chosen. One of the chosen. (*Beat.*) And look what happened to them!

'My Lords, Ladies and Gentlemen. I had an aunt – yes, even old women may once have had aunts – I had an aunt who while burning at the stake – well not literally but you know what I mean – said: "Betty," she said, "never be chosen, never stand out in a crowd. If you have ideas keep them to yourself, if you have opinions – suppress them. Never argue with those in charge, those in authority, those with power. Dress soberly, live modestly, don't shout or become emotional or fall in love, if you have to fall in love try to do it without passion. The majority," she said, "are mediocre and filled with such vemonous hatred they'll slice you into bloody little bloody bits of little bloody pieces. Betty Lemon," she said, "keep your nose clean and never be chosen."'

Returns to letter.

(*Reading.*) '. . . and you will be collected and delivered home to your door . . .' (*Crying out to the noose.*) What about those handicapped by their impoverished imaginations, eh? What about a dinner for *them*? Aaaaaaah! (*She's in pain.*) Mustn't get excited. 'As a socialist,' he said. Ha!

Your problem, Betty Lemon, is you never had ambition. 'Let 'em win,' you always used to say, 'who can be bothered with all that getting ahead, all that scheming and wheeling and dealing, all that skulduggery and pecking of others out of the way. Let 'em win!'

Returns to letter.

(*Reading.*) 'Dress optional . . .'

Options in life are like an inverted pyramid!

Thinks about it.

Can't bear people who say things like that.

'As a socialist,' he said. Ha!

Shall I ring my daughter? Tell her the good news? 'Daughter, guess what! Your mother's been honoured. She's been made Handicapped Woman Of The Year. I can put H.W.O.Y. after my name. I'm a hwoy! Lady Betty Lemon – hwoy!

Giggles and drives her chair to lounge where phone sits. Has second thoughts.

Probably just get her answering machine. 'I'm not here.' Only people I ever speak to these days are answering-machines. All got their own personalities, though. Some sing, some play music, some make jokes. My daughter's machine is sparse. 'I'm not here.' A machine of a few words.

Lady Betty Lemon – hwoy! (*Giggles.*)

'As a socialist,' he said. Ha!

Coffee-time, I think.

> *She drives to kitchen area. Preparations for making coffee are another of the day's battles, for it is real coffee made from beans which she grinds in a noisy machine, and then filters.*
>
> *It is not possible to carry this out from a sitting position. She has to stand and leave her chair.*
>
> *Her first moves are: fill kettle and plug in to boil; then uncoil plug wrapped around coffee machine, plug in; next, to fridge where packet of beans, sellotaped, are kept cool. Unpicking the sellotape presents its own problems.*
>
> *As she struggles she talks.*

'As a socialist,' he said. Ha! He called everybody who disagreed with him a socialist. You only had to complain to my uncle about rent or rates going up and he'd kiss: 'Socialisssst!'

'But, uncle,' I'd say, because after a while I'd just enjoy winding him up, 'but, uncle, if cutting profits are a *dis*incentive to industrialists how can cutting wages be an *incentive* to workers?'

(*Hissing.*) 'Socialisssst!'

(*Enjoying herself.*) 'Let 'em win!' I'd yell at him.

'Spineless!' he'd yell back, his eyes popping out of his

head, the pitch of his voice rising, the words swimming about in his mouth. 'Flabby! Woolly-minded!' Ha ha! 'Let 'em win!'

(*Hissing.*) 'Socialisssst!'

(*Crying out to the noose.*) And what about those handicapped by ignorant teachers and bigoted parents. What about them?

'I'm not here.' Lady Betty Lemon – hwoy! (*Giggles.*)

> *The chair moves away from her. She watches it with disbelief and anger.*

You as well?! Come back here! At once! Now!

> *It backs away again.*

> *She hobbles towards it. It backs away. She hobbles another step. It backs away.*

> *They are developing a relationship.*

What's the matter, chair? Too heavy for you? (*Chair moves.*) Upsetting to have a smelly old woman sitting on you. (*Chair moves.*) Well no one enjoys being sat upon I can understand that but, we've all been put on this earth to serve a function and you're luckier than most: you know what yours is.

> *It backs away again.*

Be a good chair, don't give a venerable, crippled old lady a hard time in the evening of her life. I know you were made for better things than wheeling a cantankerous hag around her squalid flat but think of it this way: she's been crowned Handicapped Queen for a night and you're her throne.

> *The chair sidles away.*

Not convinced?

Chair sidles away once more.

I'll put my daughter on to you. A woman of few words and much action, my daughter.

Chair sidles away even further.

You want to get the better of me don't you? Decrepit, malfunctioning, full of wheezes, but I go on and on and on and on and it makes you mad, eh? She should be dead you're thinking. Why does she linger? Who's interested in *her*? Who cares what *she* does, what she feels, what she thinks. Get it over and done with! Sing praises! Bury her! Give the barmy old battleaxe a tomb and flowers. Goodbye, Betty Lemon. Farewell you irritating old fart.

'Rubbish!' he said, 'they all talk rubbish!'

An idea occurs to her. Perhaps if she pretends she's not interested in the chair it will stand still.

Can't let life's little irritations keep me from my coffee.

Returns to making coffee. The beans must be poured into the grinder. Inevitably they spill into the sink. She meticulously retrieves each bean.

'As a socialist.' Ha!

Was I ever really a socialist? I called myself one in those days because in those days there was no other name for what I believed. But – ssssh! Don't let on. I never joined! Wasn't a joiner. Couldn't accept majority decisions. Never really liked the majority. Not like Sir James. He loved them.

We once went on a goodwill mission to East Germany. Visited a small industrial town. Can't remember the name but I'll never forget the scene. The local councillors gave us tea. Five of *them* neatly dressed in suits of lifeless greys and browns and blues on one side of a long table, Sir James and Lady Betty Lemon from Dalston Junction with their interpreter on the other side, and little sandwiches in between, all set in a clean, polished, bleak room with photos of grim men on the cream walls. And I remember asking: 'Why are all your left-wing leaders looking to the right?' No one thought that funny.

The chief councillor was the first to speak. 'I come from the working class,' he said. 'I love the working class.' It was how he said the word 'love' that fascinated me. Urgently. Anxiously. Protestingly. 'I luuuve the working class, I luuuve them.' Methought he did protest too much as though warding them off. Calming them. He didn't 'luuuve' them. He was terrified of them.

> *The beans are in the grinder. Press button. Loud noise. Stop.*

(*Crying out to the noose.*) And what about those handicapped by weak minds? What about them?

> *She must now pour ground coffee into small filter pot and pour in hot water.*

They say yesterday's whores are today's nuns. (*Beat.*) Or is it: today's nuns were yesterday's whores? (*Beat.*) Or perhaps it's: today's whores are tomorrow's nuns? (*Beat.*) Can't bear people who say things like that.

On the other hand, you see those crowds on television and it doesn't matter what country they're in or what they're demonstrating about, their faces all have the same expression – simplistic fervour. Self-intoxicated. No thought. They've persuaded themselves their ends will be achieved *now*! At this moment! Repeat the screaming, that'll do it. Clench your fist, that'll bring the millennium.

'Rubbish!' he said, 'they all talk rubbish!'

'Ollymollycollywolly OUT OUT OUT! Thingymeejig and wadjamacallim OUT OUT OUT!'

Like a magic incantation. Their eyes ablaze with self-satisfaction. They've made a better world. Today!

'Ollymollycollywolly OUT OUT OUT! Thingymeejig and wadjamacallim OUT OUT OUT!' While far away . . . alone . . . in a cold land . . . a man lives out his existence frozen for saying 'no!'.

(*Crying out to the noose.*) And what about those handicapped by demagogues, charlatans, charismatic politicians? What about them?

> *Pours her coffee. Moves with it towards armchair in study.*

I fought them, ha! didn't I fight them. That's why Sir James turned to other women, I saw through him. '*You* play to the gallery,' I told him, 'easy solutions and slick slogans. The politics of comfort! Questions, questions! You didn't teach them to ask questions. You're filled with lies and bullshit,' I told him, 'with rubbish!' (*Beat.*) Not easy to sleep beside a woman who bites the hand that feeds her.

> *Puts coffee on a desk.*

An anarchist, that's what I really am. Elderly Handicapped Anarchist Of The Year, that's me.

(*Raising stick.*) 'Ollymollycollywolly OUT OUT OUT! Thingymeejig and wadjamacallim OUT OUT OUT!'

> *Lunges with stick at chair which anticipates her and moves away.*
>
> *She falls forward landing with great pain.*

You stupid lump of manufacture! Do as you're told! You're not made to have a life of your own, you're made to serve. To serve me. Jesus Christ! Why doesn't anything work as I want it to? Not the chair, not my bowels, not my legs, not memory, not brains! Piss bugger shit fuck why is nothing easy in this life?!

She struggles to lean against desk. Reaches for coffee. Drinks.

Good coffee. Only the best for the century's cripple.

'My Lords, Ladies and Gentlemen, I wasn't always like this . . .'

Were you not, Betty Lemon? Didn't you always let them win? (*Beat.*) Well, that was the only way to show contempt for the competitors wasn't it? 'Let 'em win!' I used to drive a car believe me or believe me not and there was never a journey without meeting some little smart-ass at the lights who'd grin at me through his window and rev his engine. He wanted to be first off on the yellow, see? And what did *you* do, Lady Lemon? You revved to make him *think* you were competing and then when the lights changed – you stayed stock-still. Made the little smart-ass really smart.

(*Crying out to the noose.*) Let 'em win! Let the relentless silly buggers win!

'I'm not here.' Lady Betty Lemon, hwoy.

A memory strikes her.

Thirteen-year-olds. They were only pathetic little thirteen-year-olds. Life still bewildered them. I can see them. They keep looking to the side checking they're doing it right. And what are they doing? Training to die! Thirteen-year-olds. Their noses are running, their eyes bulge. I can see them. On the TV screen. Some

fanatical religious war in the Middle East. Listen to
their officers. 'They're not afraid to die because when
they die it'll only be for a short time.' Don't believe me?
Listen. 'This life is only a preparation. The real one is
to follow. They will be instant martyrs in heaven.'
Fucking hallelujah! Thank Christ the grave is silent.
You can invent what you like – heaven, hell, new lives,
new beginnings. And there they stand. Thirteen-year-
olds! In rows of three. Blazing eyes. Clenched fists.
Fervour. (*Peering.*) Except . . . except (*Points.*) him!
That little one there. Look at him. He doesn't believe
them. He's pulled away. Backed up against a wall. He's
crying. 'No! No! Not me! Not me!' Go on, little one.
Cry! Cry for your life! Tell them! 'Not me! Not me!
Rubbish! You all talk rubbish!'

I shall never forget that picture. *He* wasn't a joiner.
Little mite. They should have a dinner for him.

Wonder what his name was? Wonder if they made him
go? Wonder if he died, went to heaven?

> *Whirring clock strikes the half hour.*

(*Gently, like a lamentation for the dead.*) 'Ollymollycollywolly out out out! Thingymeejig and wadjamacallim
out out out!'

(*Angrily crying at the noose.*) And what about those
handicapped by fear of their priests? What about them?

You won't go to heaven Lady Betty Lemon. Too much
bile and blasphemy burning *you* up. No reverence for
anything.

> *She raises herself. The chair moves towards her as
> though in sympathy. She stretches out her arm to
> receive it, grateful. It backs away again. She ignores
> it with dignity, sits instead in an armchair.*

Well, *there* goes another half hour I won't ever be able to live again. (*Beat.*) Can't bear people who say things like that.

'My Lords, Ladies and Gentlemen, my life was spent on many battlefronts . . .'

(*To noose.*) If only they'd known my father. *He* wasn't one of the world's joiners, either. 'Ach!' he'd say, 'they all talk rubbish and make me sick.' Dalston Junction was full of people who talked rubbish and made him sick. 'Separate them into individuals,' he said, 'they're nicer. Collect them together and you have collective madness.' Probably inherited my dislike of the majority from him. Lovely man. Everything hurt him.

Shakes herself from reverie.

'My Lords, Ladies and Gentlemen. I had a father – yes, even old women may once have had fathers – I had a father who advised me to be a writer and write rubbish. "Write rubbish," he advised, "write rubbish, make a fortune and keep us in our old age." But I didn't want to be a writer, not even one who made a fortune writing rubbish. I wanted to be, believe me or believe me not, a runner. Yes! Once I could run. Once I could swim, dive, the high jump, the long jump, leap over hurdles. An athlete! That's what *I* wanted to be, my Lords, Ladies and Gentlemen, not a writer but a runner who won races. I was neither. I became a wife. To Sir James.'

(*Crying out to the noose.*) What about those handicapped by the wrong relationship until death do them part? What about them?

She thinks she hears something.

What was that? I heard a voice. There was movement.

Who's there? Is that you, Mother? She always said she'd come back. 'And when I do don't be frightened.'

Why not? Why shouldn't I be frightened? Give me one good reason why I shouldn't be frightened?

Long pause.

She once threw a pile of spoons at me. She did! We're sitting down to a meal and she asks me to go upstairs and bring down two chairs to the table. My brothers are there and I ask her 'Why don't *they* bring them down?' 'Because I asked *you*,' she replies. 'Well I won't,' I say, 'not while there are two big hefty boys standing idle either side of me.' So she throws the spoons.

She looks around, listens.

Mother, are you carrying spoons?

I don't *really* believe she's out there. Or that anyone is out there. That's another of your problems, Betty Lemon – you're not a believer.

Phone rings.

She struggles to her feet knowing she won't make it in time, cursing like a child.

Piss bugger shit fuck! Piss bugger shit fuck! Piss bugger shit fuck!

She arrives just as the phone stops ringing.

Probably my daughter. She always rings while I'm otherwise engaged. Does it deliberately. 'Mother is moving her bowels, let's ring her.'

She dials. Waits.

We hear the phone ring followed by the whirr of a message-machine going into action. Her daughter's recorded voice-over.

DAUGHTER'S VOICE. I'm not here. If –

BETTY *slams down phone angrily.*

BETTY. Of course you're not there! Can't I hear you're not fucking there! She's worked out this message specially to annoy me. No 'This is 262 2134' so's you know you've got the right number. No 'I'm *sorry* we're not here' or 'I'm *sorry* we're working' or 'I'm *sorry* we're not in the mood for speaking to people.' Nothing! 'They know my voice,' she says. But what if someone needs you urgently who *doesn't* know your voice?

She dials again.

Again the –

DAUGHTER'S VOICE. I'm not here. If you want to leave a message speak after the tone.

Tone. Again angrily slams down phone.

BETTY. Not even '*Please* speak after the tone and I'll ring you back.' Sparse. She's very sparse, my daughter. Now *she* wants to be a writer. A sparse writer.

(*Crying out to the noose.*) What about those handicapped by talent, taste, a touch of colour, style? What about them?

'You want to be a writer?' I tell her, 'write rubbish or they'll crucify you.' (*Imitating the diminishers.*) 'Who does she think she is? Takes herself too seriously that's her trouble.'

'Write rubbish,' I yell at her, 'write rubbish, make a fortune and keep me in my old age.' Not her. 'I'm not here.' Uncompromising. 'I'm not here.' A sparse writer. 'I'm not here.' You can't be more sparse than that.

Dials again.

DAUGHTER'S VOICE. I'm not here. If you want to leave a message speak after the tone.

BETTY. Hello, machine. And how are you today? (*Beat.*) Can't talk? Not feeling well? Feeling depressed? Well one thing *you'll* never have to endure: speaking into the fucking void.

Hello, daughter. This is your Handicapped Mother Of The Year calling you from heaven. I passed away two months ago. You can reach me on cloud nine extension 010101010101 . . . Oh! Oh! Oh!

> *She is in tears.*

> *Controls herself.*

Goodbye, machine.

> *Receiver down.*

(*Calling out to the noose.*) And what about those handicapped by despair? What about them?

> *She wanders around her flat. Lost. Lonely. Uncertain what to do, where to settle. Finds herself beneath the noose. Utterly depressed.*

One thing I never was – sparse. There was something mean about being sparse – a tight-lipped malice, a thin envy, a grudging rebuke. *I* was never grudging, envious, mean. Touch of malice now and then, can't help that in this life, but – careful? Never. Sir James was. Trod carefully. Loved carefully. Carefully approved of and hated the right people, the marked groups, the listed causes. Not a hair or a word out of place, not a decibel above par. Me – I chased and screamed him around the globe, took emotional risks, asked unfashionable questions. Fatal! But to *him* they gave a knighthood. (*Beat.*) And kept him out of the Cabinet. My fault. All my fault. Everything my fault. I let 'em win.

'My Lord, Ladies and Gentlemen. I had a mother – yes, even old women may once have had mothers – I had a mother, a strong and tiny thing she was who gave me two pieces of advice. "Talk," she said, "always *say* it. Something is remembered." And once, when I was rude and she was upset, I told her "but I was only joking". "There are no jokes. Nobody," she said, "makes jokes." '

> *An idea comes to her. She raises her stick to pull down the noose.*

> *She is going to use it to lasso her wheelchair! What follows depends upon the power for comic invention of the actress and director. Whatever that is, she finally succeeds. The chair is hers again. She sits there exhausted but triumphant.*

> *The feeling of triumph is brief.*

'My Lords, Ladies and Gentlemen. I wasn't always like this. I . . .'

'My Lords, Ladies and Gentlemen. My life was spent on many battlefronts which . . .'

'My Lords, Ladies and Gentlemen. We are given but one life, and . . .'

'My Lords, Ladies and Gentlemen . . .

. . . I didn't fucking plan it this way.'

> *Whirring clock strikes eight.*

> *Slow fade of lights.*

The Mistress

On Passover night the youngest child asks:

'Wherefore is this night different from all other nights. . . ?'

And the father replies:

'Once were we slaves in Egypt and the Lord our God brought us forth from thence with a mighty hand and an outstretched arm . . .'

The Mistress was first performed on 18 November 1991 at the Piccolo Teatro di Arezzo, Italy, and then in the Flaiano Theatre, Rome, on 23 November 1991, with Claretta Carotenuto, directed by Arnold Wesker and designed by Hilary Baxter. Its first UK production was on 24 September 1997 in a double-bill with *Break, My Heart* at the Sherman Theatre, Cardiff, with Denise Black, directed by Michael Bogdanov and designed by Ulrike Engelbrecht.

When Samantha talks to herself she will be named Samantha. When she is engaged in exchanges with the dummies she will be named Babushka. But only Ninotchka will call her Babushka, Jessica will call her Sam or Samantha. This will become clear.

The play takes place over three hours from 7.30 in the evening until 10.30. Time passes between sections indicated by asterisks.

SAMANTHA'S MELODY

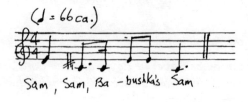

Sam, Sam, Ba-bushka's Sam

Corner of a dress-designer's atelier.

Although there is a desk, a swivel chair, phone – the main atmosphere is created by the paraphernalia of a workshop the main part of which is off-stage.

The space had once been used for something else – warehouse, engineering works – architectural features of which remain.

What we see are:

– raised platform on which sits a cutting-table
– rolls of coloured cloth and lining beneath it
– nearby a tailor's dummy unclad
– ironing-board
– an overlock machine fed by coons of coloured nylon thread which stretch across space like a Hepworth abstract sculpture
– racks upon which hang finished clothes
– garments in various stages of completion, and samples of material which stand out against a wall
– a battery of pegs on which are 'plugged' cotton-reels of every possible hue
– drawings, sketches, cuttings from fashion magazines pinned on boards
– a sewing-machine tailing off and hinting at many more off-stage
– two more tailor's dummies upon which are draped startling but unfinished dresses.

The atmosphere of this workshop is flushed by shape, texture and a mosaic blaze of colour.

Two mottos like graffiti on different parts of the wall give us the first hint of the woman we are about to see:

'KNOCK HARD. LIFE IS DEAF.'

'NO GOOD DEED GOES UNPUNISHED.'

SAMANTHA MILNER – *nicknamed 'Babushka' – enters humming to herself 'Sam, Sam, Babushka's Sam . . .',* a pile of magazines in her arms, keys in her hand, dressed in what could be described as 'The Russian Look':*

voluminous skirt, embroidered blouse, peasant waistcoat, boots, hat. Obviously her own creation.

On the end of her nose – thick, black-rimmed half-glasses.

She is thirty-nine years old, voluptuous, energetic, efficient, talented and famous. Her parents were Eastern European émigrés but she has no accent. Just a rhythm of speech.

What to put down first? Keys or magazines? Thinks to put magazines on cutting table. Wrong place. So, keys – into desk drawer. Then, where to put the magazines? Not on desk, too cluttered. Looks around. Ah! under cutting-table – for the moment.

Decisions! Every moment brings decisions.

Raises her hat to the clad dummies.

SAMANTHA. 'Evening, girls!

– and on the unclad one places it.

My, but you look beautiful this evening. Where *did* you get those stunning dresses?

Approaching between them, peeling off her clothes.

Are we going to have a nice quiet evening together? Catch up on work? Answer the 'appeal' letters? No insolence, no back-chat, no blinding questions?

Moves from them to hang scarf and coat on a rack.

---

* 'Babushka' is Russian for 'grandmother'. Sam is nicknamed 'Babushka' because she was her grandmother's favourite. Her notes are a melody she composed as a child to comfort herself.

You're talking to the dummies, Sam. You promised yourself you'd *stop* talking to the dummies, Sam.

She promised herself many things didn't she, Jessica? To stop drinking, to cut out chocolates, to say 'no' more often to clients, to give *him* up.

(*Innocently.*) To give who up?

Him, Samantha, him! 'Who'! God, you're so full of shit.

> *Moves to Jessica. An alteration is required.*

> *She reaches up to 'sculpture' to snap off two different shades of blue cotton.*

> *Holds them against Jessica's dress.*

Decisions! Decisions! Decisions!

> *Decides on one shade, hangs it over dummy's shoulder.*

There! Better! Better, Jessica? Better!

> *Turns to second dummy.*

You, Ninotchka, I'm *not* so sure about. You looked good on the drawing board but on your feet? No, don't cry. It's probably something very simple. (*Beat.*) Like starting from scratch.

> *Moves to a drawing pad. Flicks through pages. A sketch catches her eye.*

> *She walks aside to get a better view of Ninotchka.*

I'll try. I'm not promising anything.

> *Draws. Considers. Something wrong. Makes a change. Worse. Puts huge X across the page.*

Cursi! Cursi, cursi, cursi! (*Pronounced like 'pussy'. This word will be explained later.*)

The phone rings.

She stiffens but doesn't move. Looks at her watch.

That's not you. It can't be you. It's only 7.34.

Rings on.

You're a client. A rich, impatient, thoughtlessly-demanding client who forgot she has a wedding in two days' time and needs the most beautiful outfit in the world. Yesterday!

Rings on.

It *can't* be you. (*Pause.*) You're a client inviting me to one of your hen parties. I hate hen parties. You'll talk about your diets, your husbands, your children, your homes in that order and I'm not interested. I am *not*!

Phone stops.

Thank you. (*Pause.*) Or *was* it you? Christ! (*Continues drawing.*) We make plans, maps, sign-codes, language codes, time-schedules; we invent one-act plays with imaginary dialogue and still nothing is predictable.

Phone rings again.

It *can't* be you. We agreed nine o'clock.

Rings on.

You're a client on my blacklist ringing to apologise for passing me a dud cheque. (*Beat.*) Or the one who tried to haggle on the agreed price. (*Beat.*) You're one of the crude, the cruel, the know-alls, the bargainers, the bloody-minded, the really nasty ones and you're ringing to say it won't ever happen again, you're a new woman, your life's changed.

It rings on.

Well I don't believe you.

Phone stops.

No one ever changes.

She's waiting for the phone-call for which she always waits but is pretending to herself that she's come to work.

She is designing a Spanish-style flamenco dress and is going to draw parts of it on the brown paper she unrolls from a roll attached to the end of her cutting-table. She will cut them out later.

Measuring and drawing:

Change, Jessica? Let me tell you about change. Change is when white becomes black, a woman becomes a man, a Chinaman becomes an Englishman. But the insensitive do *not* become sensitive, the ugly do *not* become beautiful, and the foolish do *not* become wise. Believe me! An insurance agent may become a farmer after thirty years but that's not change, that's finding other parts of yourself.

The phone rings. Moves to it swiftly.

On the other hand you could be five thousand pounds.

Answers in a French accent.

SAMANTHA *is a raconteur, a mimic, an entertaining 'performer' for her friends.*

'Ello? Zee residence of Miss Samantha Milner. (*Pause.*) No, I am not she. I am zee cleaning lady and I assure you zis place needs very cleaning. 'Oo is zat plise? (*Pause.*) Ah, Lady Madley. Well she cannot see you zis evening because she is not 'ere. Even zee wicked must rest. (*Pause.*) No, no. A French proverb. (*Pause.*) Your son is what? (*Incredulous.*) Getting engaged in two days' time? (*Laughing.*) You want zat Samantha Milner make for you (*Laughs.*) in two days . . . ? (*Laughs.*) Yes, I tell 'er. I don't know what she say but I will tell 'er. Excuse I laugh, I just woman who cleans but even zee peasant can dig a straight line. No, no. Obscure French proverb. Merci! Au revoir.

I know what she'll fucking say. She'll say go to Harrods or Paris or make it yourself. Better still, she'll say it'll cost a thousand more. Be exclusive! Right, Ninotchka? Hard to get! Right, Jessica? Make it difficult for them to buy you – that way you're appreciated, sought after, better paid.

> *Now that she is at her desk she catches sight of a pile of mail that seems to have been specially put aside. She picks up top sheets.*

Appeals, appeals, appeals! As if I didn't have *enough* to make me feel guilty.

★   ★   ★

> *She glances at the appeals one by one. It's her habit to make a decision from four or five at a time.*

(*Reading.*) 'The Samaritans. . .'
'Writers and Scholars Education Trust for Free Speech.'
'Friends of the Earth . . . Dear Miss Milner, you are one of a number of respected public figures we are asking to adopt a thousand trees in a Brazilian rain forest. I expect you are approached every day with a request to help a charity or to give to some worthy cause. Let me explain . . .'

> *She sits. Reaches for a cheque book in drawer.*

No need to explain. I'll 'adopt' a thousand trees.

(*Writing.*) 'Friends . . . of . . . the . . . Earth . . . twenty-five . . . pounds.' There! so a few more wild flowers can survive. An exotic lizard or two.

She places rejects on floor beside her, and begins to stack those she responds to. Everything becomes a ritual for her.

Takes up another bunch of papers.

'Celebrities Guild of Great Britain . . . tickets for the Gala dinner . . . awards to unsung heroes . . .'
Tell me, Ninotchka, who is *not* an unsung hero?
'Royal Society for Mentally Handicapped Children and Adults . . .'
'Nightingale House for the Jewish Aged . . .'
'National Society for Epilepsy . . .'

Decisions! Decisions! Decisions! God help me, Jessica. Whose suffering do I choose first?

No blinding questions, Sam. We promised ourselves no blinding questions this evening.

That's not a real blinding question, Jessica, that's what's known in the business of living as a rhetorical question.

Reaching for cheque book.

There's a rumour you've got Jewish blood in your family, Sam. (*Writing.*) Nightingale . . . Home . . . for . . . the . . . Jewish . . . Aged . . . twenty-five pounds. Wait! There's a blinding rumour that one day you'll grow old, Sam. Make it fifty.

Rejects to floor. Add accepted letter to pile.

From another desk drawer she pulls out a whisky glass, and from yet another – a half-filled bottle of Jack Daniel's whisky.

(*Pouring.*) I think it's the inevitable letter I dread.

The melody of this letter is always the same.

'My Dear Samantha,' it will begin, 'you have made me realise I love my wife . . .'

Drinks.

(*Pouring a second glass.*) I also love his wife. My good friend! What's that got to do with anything? (*Drinks.*)

* * *

I can remember how we first met. He gave a lecture. On women's clothes: 'The exposure of the mind by the concealment of the body.' How could I not go? Wasn't even his field. Historian of the Victorian years with a curiosity for clothes on the side. Dreadful organisers, dreadful hostess. I phoned. 'You are very bored,' I told him without introducing myself. 'Those people you are with are the killers of all time. I'm having a party. Come and join me. I'll put you right about women's clothes.' A dark voice from out the night. Adventure! Nothing like that had ever happened to him. 'How will I know you?' he asked. 'You will know me,' I replied. He was so beautiful. (*Pause.*) And so married. (*Pause.*) And to such a wonderful woman. (*Pause.*) I fell in love with her, too. (*Finishes drink.*)

> *Returns glass and bottle to their drawers. Rituals, rituals, rituals!*
>
> *Picks up sheaf of appeals.*
>
> *She's forgotten to put up her glasses. Peers. Realises she's trying to read without them.*

(*Returning glasses to nose.*) I'm going blind as well.

'Durham University Bolivia Expedition . . .'
'International Fund for Animal Welfare . . .'

'The Nicaragua Health Fund . . .'
'British Wildlife . . .'

Considers. Reaching for cheque book.

People should be healthy. (*Writing.*) The . . . Nicaragua
. . . Health . . . Fund . . . This is going to be an
expensive evening for you, Sam.

Which one of you said that? It's *my* money! All these
noble people here looking up *Who's Who*, spending
hours formulating the *best* letter to make me feel the
most guilty? They should *know* they're succeeding, that
someone out there *feels* guilty.

Moves up to continue drawing her pattern.

You're talking to the dummies again, Sam. How many
times must I tell you – talk to dummies you'll stop
believing in your*self*. Belief, Jessica? Let me tell you
about belief. Belief is believing life is more important
than belief. Belief is young and twenty and all the world
loving you. Belief is every single person with a heart of
gold, a head of brains, a sensitive soul, endless talents,
the parts in harmony if only . . . (*Longingly.*) if only, if
only ah! if only . . .

(*Dreamily.*) When I was young I wrote in my diary,
'Dear God, I don't mind what happens to me as long as
*some*thing does!'

Concentrates on drawing pattern.

The parts in harmony . . . parts, parts, parts . . .

(*Brightly.*) 'Do you know the parts of things?' he asks –
he's full of ideas for making a fortune – 'I know the
parts of a garment,' I say. 'The under-bodice back, the
under-bodice side-front, the armhole facing – that kind
of part?' 'Exactly!' he says. 'But do you know the parts
of a car, a cathedral, a flower, clouds?'

Moves from behind table to address the dummies more directly.

'You're at a shoot,' he says. 'This stunning model in your stunning creation, and your stunning setting is a stately home. "Stand her there," you say. "Where?" they ask. "By that part there," you say. "What part where?" they ask. "*That* part, the one with bits sticking out at the top . . ."' He's right! I don't know the name of the part of *any*thing. (*Returning to table.*) '*An Encyclopedia of Parts*,' he says. 'A fortune! Made for life!' He's always looking to be 'made for life'.

Draws on in silence.

'My dear Samantha,' it will begin, 'you know you will always be someone special for me, but . . .'

I hate 'buts'. 'You're right, but . . .' 'It's a beautiful dress, but . . .' 'Normally I'd die for you, but . . .'

Draws on in silence.

        ★   ★   ★

Do you enjoy being a mistress?

Who asked that? Which one of you brazen dummies asked that? Is that this evening's blinding question? 'Enjoy'? Let me tell you about 'enjoy'. 'Enjoy' is when you achieve what you set out to achieve, when you know what it is you *want* to achieve. When you have opinions, standards, a sense of history, a cultural framework so that anywhere, any time, you know what the hell is being spoken about. When everything in you is good and sweet and innocent and the parts come together, when you love your*self* rather than your good friend's husband. I tell you! 'Enjoy' is when your conscience is clear, you feel comfortable with yourself, you can look in a mirror and say 'good morning' instead of 'yeach'! I need another whisky.

To the desk. The drawers. The glass. The bottle. Drink in one go.

Picks up sheaf of appeals.

(*Reading.*) 'As you may be aware, 1998 will be the 60th Anniversary of the *Anschluss* of Austria and the *Reichskristallnacht*, the night when the first vicious attacks were made on synagogues and Jewish property in Austria and Germany . . .'

Was I aware? I was not aware. (*Beat.*) Of how much else am I not aware?
(*Reading.*) 'Timor Solidarity Campaign . . .'
'The Romanian Emergency . . .'
'Dear Miss Milner, we are writing to you about Alfonso Castiglione Mendoza, the Peruvian writer who has recently been released from prison in Russia . . .'

Spreads letters over her desk.

OK, *you* decide. Money to help commemorate human suffering? Money for democracy? Money for food? Money for an individual victim of state-oppression? And we haven't come to the end of the pile yet. A year's collection of unanswered appeals for help. They have to be faced.

★   ★   ★

Swivels to face rack of clothes.

What shall I wear for him tonight?

Rises to rack. Shuffles clothes.

Long, clinging, décolleté? Something sparkly with black

net stockings, suspenders? Decisions, decisions, decisions!

From under her cutting-table a box of perfumes.

And which perfume? Fiji? Aramis? Blazer by Anne Klein? Not really, they're for sport. Ralph Lauren? Tatiana? No, they're for day clothes. Eau de Floris by Nina Ricci? Mmm. Romantic but not sexy. Nocturnes by Caron? Paris by Yves St Laurent? Opium? I smell Opium on everyone. All day. Belongs to nightdresses actually. (*Beat.*) Don't laugh. He cares about such things.

Replaces perfumes under table.

To be honest, so do I.

During this next, looking at the unclad dummy upon which she's placed her hat, she idly transfers her coat and scarf to it as well.

I know, Jessica, he *promised* to phone but he may not be *able* to phone. He *may* be free or he may *not* be free. He *might* want to go to a theatre, a movie, a concert, a restaurant – or he might just want to *talk*.

Or not.

Make love.

Or not.

Now there is a dummy in her own image.

'Evening, Babushka. (*Sing song, lullaby.*) Sam, Sam, Babushka's Sam.

So, the dress to put stars in his eyes? The one to outline my lush curves? The stern, austere two-piece – which if the truth be known really belongs to my middle-age –

with knee-length socks to remind me I was once a schoolgirl?

Moves to hug Jessica from behind.

Oh, Jessica. Was I ever a schoolgirl? What did I *think* in those days? What did I *feel*, what did I *imagine*, what did I *want* for myself?

Play-acts 'the girls'.

Why don't you tell us, Sam?

You notice she doesn't talk to *me* much, Jessica.

Well you're such a fearsome woman, Ninotchka.

She's frightened I'll ask her a blinding question.

Ignore her, Sam. Tell us about being a young girl.

Go on, Babushka, tell us about the first time you seduced a young man.

A young boy, actually, when I was a young girl. About fifteen.

Sits on edge of rostrum between her 'girls'.

I had always dreamed of seduction. The power that comes with it. Nothing brazen, nothing coy or coquettish. I hated all that in those days. But letting him know that you longed, that you ached, that with *you* there was the possibility – your eyes, your smile, a gesture, touch, a word – ah! the confidence then.

It was at a mixed camp for the children of Russian immigrants, in a river valley. I saw this boy, beautiful, intelligent, vivid, loved being alive – bit unworldly if the truth be known. And I found all that irresistible.

He'd attached himself to another girl. Sweet and matronly. 'Wrong,' I said to myself. 'She doesn't see you,' I said to myself. 'I'm what you need, and *you*,' I said to myself, 'are what I will have.' And on the last night, when he was about to capture the embrace he'd worked so hard to achieve, she fell asleep. As sweet and matronly girls often do. And I reached out a hand which I knew he'd take and I laid it on my firm, young breast, and O how that nipple rose and carried his heat to my audacious parts. While he worked for a mere matronly kiss I had worked my alchemy to lose him deep inside me. Mmmmm!

Rises to sit at desk.

Don't get me wrong, Jessica, we were equals – me and my beautiful boy.

Swivels to face Babushka.

Only some of us, as has been recorded, are more equals than others, are we not, Babushka?

Swivels back to again consider the four appeal letters.

The individual starting a new life after prison, I think. (*Sits. Writes.*) Alfonso . . . Castiglione Mendoza . . . Fund . . . fifty pounds.

What a good safety valve. Do you think they know this, the charity-mongers? 'Let's write to Samantha Milner, unmarried, no children, she must be stealing *some-*body's husband. Loaded with guilts!' They're a bit like the police, the charity-mongers, they know we've all got something to hide.

★   ★   ★

This won't pay the bills.

Rises.

You have work to do, Sam.

Returns to drawing.

Draws on in silence.

You don't really have work to do. You have six people to work *for* you. You're just killing time, waiting.

Draws on in silence.

I can remember my *first* married lover. We made a pact. '*I* won't tell you about my other lovers and you won't tell me how much you really love your wife and children.'

Rolls back brown paper in order to begin cutting the shapes she's drawn.

But the second one – he was mean. Came for a week. Brought his own shampoo and conditioner with him. Left with the half-finished bottles. Also the half-finished bottle of cheap wine. Which finished us!

First cut.

Then there was the one who cried when it was done.

Cuts on in silence.

And the one who picked a quarrel five minutes after.

Cuts on in silence.

And the one who immediately phoned his wife to see how she was.

Cuts on in silence.

Do you think that perhaps you don't really *like* men, Babushka?

(*Fiercely.*) Is that your idea of a 'blinding question', Ninotchka? Well I think it's a stupid question and I have no time for stupid questions. I have this gorgeous flamenco dress to cut.

Pins cut-out pattern on board behind her.

Cuts on in silence.

'My dear Samantha,' it will begin, 'I suppose you knew this letter would come one day . . .'

★ ★ ★

Wanders down to desk – usually the best position from which to address the three dummies. Pours herself another drink.

Although it began as playfulness, SAMANTHA, *the more she becomes drunk, assumes the characters she has given to her dummies.*

From here on there are three characters – Jessica, Ninotchka and Babushka, with SAMANTHA *playing all of them.*

She moves, often violently, between the dummies, to 'be' them, sometimes turning Ninotchka to face upstage to Babushka, sometimes turning Jessica to face Ninotchka, like a child playing war games with lead soldiers.

NINOTCHKA. Are you an honest woman, Babushka?

JESSICA. Leave her alone, Ninotchka. Have pity on a working girl.

BABUSHKA. I'm crippled with honesty. Problem with honesty is that it inspires an excess of self-criticism which doesn't always apply.

NINOTCHKA. Come now, Babushka, you *think* you're honest. But what about all those dark corners of the soul, those hidden recesses of the mind, those delicious secrets of the heart?

Moves between them.

JESSICA. You're a spitful old hag, Ninotchka, you know that?

BABUSHKA. Thank you, Jessica. You I could always rely on to understand.

NINOTCHKA. But the question, Babushka, the one really blinding question you dare not face.

BABUSHKA. *What* question? There are no questions I daren't face. My friends *love* me at their parties for the questions I dare ask and dare answer and dare face.

NINOTCHKA. All of them?

BABUSHKA. *All* of them!

NINOTCHKA. She's not being honest now is she, Jessica?

JESSICA. Ninotchka, you're overstepping the mark.

BABUSHKA. Thank you, Jessica.

Ninotchka turns on Babushka upstage.

NINOTCHKA. *You* think the wife should feel proud don't you, Babushka? On the one hand proud that she's not married to a timid, faithful, spineless wimp but to a man who dares and is dazzling – which is a reflection of her; and on the other hand proud that no mistress has been good enough to take him away from her. Only one thing wrong with that isn't there, Babushka? (*To Jessica.*) The wife's become her good friend!

JESSICA (*to Babushka*). Then why him, Sam? Your good friend's husband? Why him?

BABUSHKA (*desperately*). Because, Jessica, he doesn't compete with me. He's the most balanced man I know. He listens, he explains, he asks questions, he can change his mind. I feel safe with him, looked after, special in his life. He has a still centre and – and –

NINOTCHKA (*up to Babushka*). Oh, be honest, Babushka. The sex is lascivious and breathtaking! God! She's so full of shit! She makes it sound so virtuous.

(*Down to Jessica.*) Virtue, Jessica? Let me tell you about virtue and the ease with which one lies feeling no guilt whatsoever. Let me tell you about virtue and the ease with which one is devious and expects virtue from others. Let me tell you about the virtuous heart that can harden while the rest remains soft, sweet and tender – because let there be no misunderstanding, Babushka is all these things – a fine and lovely and virtuous person, except in this one respect: she lies to her good friend with the talent of a sublime actress. Her good friend whom she loves – and let there be no misunderstanding about that either, her good friend can ask her life of her but – when she had her good friend's husband in her arms, on her lips and between those ample, fleshy thighs her good friend is banished from her thoughts. They no longer exist for each other. Now (*Turning Jessica to face upstage to Babushka.*) ask her how. How, Sam, how can this be?

Waits.

She won't answer? Then I'll tell you how this can be, my dear sister. Because real joy, real happiness, the joy and happiness that love brings is not only fleeting, it's rare. You may never be given another chance. Virtue, betrayal, loyalty, guilt, all pale, fade, are as nothing to that ecstasy which may never come again.

She wanders up to her work at the cutting-table.

The play-acting dies away as this last is uttered in her own voice.

SAMANTHA. Imagine! To live only once and never, never taste that ecstasy. Imagine!

★ ★ ★

The evening's light has faded.

She regards one of her pattern shapes on the brown paper.

Time has passed. He hasn't phoned.

She flicks switch on wall. Workshop light.

Did I draw this? Couldn't have been concentrating.

She tears off pattern shape, pulls out more paper from roll at end of table.

BABUSHKA. My daddy wanted me to be an academic. A thinker! Wanted me to add at least one original thought to the world. But I didn't have an original thought. Not even one. 'I want to be a dress designer, Daddy,' I said. 'I want to make women look beautiful.' 'Cursi!' he yelled at me. 'Beauty comes from what people *are*, not what they wear. Cursi, cursi, cursi!' 'What,' I asked him, 'does "cursi" mean?'

And he told me a story.

(*To Jessica.*) In Venezuela there lived a bourgeois family by the name of Sicur. They had three daughters who were very arrogant and pretentious, and said things like 'Oh look at the moon, how it moves my soul.' And 'I love music, it makes me weepy.' And 'When I have a baby it will be the pride of my life.'

Moves to desk for another whisky.

Nearly everyone was impressed by the Sicur sisters and they were invited to parties where all the other young women tried to be like them and invent things to say which could be accompanied by significant sighs. One evening, at just such a party, a young woman was heard to say in a loud voice 'Oh, how mysterious the nights are.' At which a young man, who hated the Sicur sisters, cried out so that they heard 'Oh my God, another cursi!' The word stuck. Cur-si, Si-cur, cursi! Kitsch of the heart! And my father, who himself wanted to add an original thought to the world but failed, warned me in life against many kinds of cursi. 'Beware,' he said 'of cursi of the heart, the hearth, and the intellect.'

He hated people who said such things as 'There's nothing like a fire to make a room feel homely.' '*Domestic* cursi!' cried my father.

He despised those who defended religious dogma with facile arguments. 'But can you prove there *isn't* a God? Can you prove there *isn't* a life after this one?' '*Intellectual* cursi!' screamed my father.

> *Returns to between 'the girls'.*

I brought home a young man once, from art college. 'This is my father,' I introduced them. 'Daddy, this is James. He's studying sculpture.' My father didn't like him. His eyes, they kept moving. 'I hope there's no nonsense going on between you.' He always came quickly to the point, my father. James was incredulous. 'I believe,' said James with hard skin on his hands, 'in sexual friendships.' 'Cursi of the *heart!*' exploded my father. 'Cursi, cursi, cursi!'

SAMANTHA. 'My dear Samantha,' it will begin, 'there is a corner of my heart that will forever be . . .'

★ ★ ★

NINOTCHKA. Notice, Jessica, she hasn't answered that question about not really *liking* men.

Down to stand by desk. Desk light on.

SAMANTHA. Stop this, Sam. Madness! You're letting two dummies rule your life.

Picks up sheaf of appeals.

'Gay Sweatshop Theatre Company . . .'
'Index Against Censorship . . .'
'Marie Curie Cancer Care . . .'
'Action for Justice . . . accountability in government . . .'

Pause.

Decisions, decisions, decisions! If only I believed in God everything would be easier. Confessors, explanations, certitudes, a moral centre that held the parts . . .

NINOTCHKA. Well, none of *us* is going to paradise that's for sure. Purgatory for us. The half-way house. Where each of us will be given the one task we loathe most on earth. You hate ironing? You'll be made to iron. You hate scrubbing floors? You'll be made to scrub floors. You hate washing up? You'll be made to wash up. Especially pots of burnt meat.

JESSICA. Have more sympathy for her, Ninotchka.

NINOTCHKA (viciously). Why?

JESSICA. She's *your* bread and butter too, you know.

NINOTCHKA. 'Not by bread alone!'

JESSICA. Oh you're full of such cursi cant, Ninotchka.

NINOTCHKA. Very good, Jessica. Cursi cant! Witty! Yes, I like that. Cursi cant!

Pause.

SAMANTHA. 'My dear Samantha,' it will begin, 'I cannot live any longer with the guilt . . .'

★ ★ ★

She storms at Babushka.

SAMANTHA. Stop this! Stop it, stop it! There is a dearth of poets. You'll never find another like him. Get on your knees.

Swiftly down to be Ninotchka.

NINOTCHKA. Oh my! How apocalyptically she speaks. But how easy it is for such as you to grab the poets, Babushka. Glamorous career, energy, friends, a large Slavic family of brothers, sisters, cousins, uncles, aunts . . . you live in this glorious city of political activity and intellectual stimulation and a dozen arts and a thou-sand-and-one culinary delights but – what about the poor provincial woman whose passion is stormy but whose horizons are hedges? The suburban wife who discovered literature at a suburban school and finds her transformed suburban imagination falling on stony suburban ground? What advice do you have for them? The wife who's made a mistake? The middle-aged spinster who can see it all passing by? The desperate widows? The sixty-year-olds who as we all know are dormant volcanoes? You who have rationalised your treachery, what advice do you have for them?

BABUSHKA. Well, well, Ninotchka. Is that your blinding question? Based on cheap guilt? (*Moving to desk.*) You want me to respond to other people's mistakes when here I'm confronted with *real* misfortune – misery perpetrated by man and nature? You'll have to do better than that, Ninotchka darling.

Glancing at latest batch.

SAMANTHA. 'Action for Justice' I think.

Sits, pulls cheque book to her.

Accountability in government. (*Writing.*) Action for Justice . . . seventy-five pounds . . .

Another drawer. A box of chocolates. Which one?

Decisions, decisions, decisions!

Picks one and eats.

The great Russian dancer Pavlova said, 'Artists should know all about love – and learn to live without it.'

Returns box to drawer.

★ ★ ★

BABUSHKA. And then there was the lover who sang given any pretext. He'd see a shop called 'Daisy's' and he'd say 'Oh look, a shop called Daisy's.' (*Sings.*) 'Daisy, Daisy, give me your answer, do . . .'

En route to cutting-table.

Then the winter came and I complained of the cold. (*Sings.*) 'Your tiny hand is frozen, let me warm it close in mine . . .'

Preparing to cut.

Once we passed an ecclesiastical bookshop in New York called 'The Hallelujah Bookstore' – 'DON'T!' I warned.

Cuts.

Tantalising pause, as if the 'girls' wait.

JESSICA. And did he, Sam, did he, did he?

Arms in the air, with gusto – sings:

BABUSHKA. HA–LLELUJAH! HA–LLELUJAH! Hallelujah! Hallelujah! Ha – lay – ey – lu – ja.

I have had them all.

What *shall* I wear for him tonight?

She moves to rack, selects skirt and top for ironing.

This!

Moves with them to ironing-board. Switches on iron. Waits. She will only ever iron the skirt.

NINOTCHKA. Notice once more, sister, the artful way Babushka has avoided all the questions? Like all these letters of appeal which she kept putting aside? But there's still one blinding question waiting isn't there, Babushka? One you can't avoid any more than you can avoid the world's cries or the cries of –

SAMANTHA. Phone! Phone! It's gone nine o'clock. Phone!

Swiftly to cutting-table drawer in which there is another box of chocolates.

A chocolate. I need a chocolate or two. Let me see now. Which one shall I have next? Decisions, decisions, decisions! Burnt sugar crunch in truffle? Roast almonds in cream? Soft toffee between biscuit? Oh look, a Jack Daniel's liqueur.

Bites. Breathes deeply. Sits squat-legged on cutting-table.

★   ★   ★

There was one lover I met at a dinner party who was very reluctant to begin a conversation. He seemed – I can't describe it any other way – to flinch from it, as though knowing that inevitably the question would come: what do *you* do for a living? 'Oh, nothing interesting,' he said. I pressed. 'Not as interesting as *your* profession,' he resisted. He'd obviously devised many ways of trying to fend off the reply. 'Come,' I said, 'it must be or you wouldn't be at this table.' I'm in manufacture,' he said at last. I waited. 'Some people,' I said, 'would be satisfied with that reply. Not me I'm afraid. I am as you know relentless. What *kind* of manufacture?' He capitulated. 'Toilet paper,' he replied.

Well, I understood. It *was* very difficult to know what to say after that. And I could see him watching me, closely, as though he judged people by the way they responded. It was unnerving. Some I suppose would exaggerate their interest. 'Toilet paper? Oh, *really?*' Some probably splutter all over the place. 'Toilet paper? Ah – oh – mmm – yeeeees – weeeeellll . . .' Most people probably change the subject as soon as they can. 'Toilet paper? And do you have children?'

Me, I was to the point. Tough old Sam. 'Toilet paper?' I said. 'And is there much competition?' You should have seen his little face light up. 'As a matter of fact,' he said, 'there is. From Korea. They make it much more cheaply than we can.' 'Ah,' I asked quick as a lizard, 'but is it as good?' 'Oh no,' he cried, and we spent another half-hour on the technical problems involved in the manufacture of that without which life can be complicated, and the rest of the evening on the counter-productiveness of terrorism, on music, literature, love, sexual politics, his place or my place and many other things without which life would be complicated.

Returns to iron in silence.

★ ★ ★

NINOTCHKA. And babies?

Irons in silence.

And babies?

Irons in silence.

And babies?

BABUSHKA. You are relentless!

OK. You want to know about babies? Let me tell you about babies. I don't relate to them. I don't understand why they're not adults. I don't understand why they're there, crying, smelling, demanding, helpless. I get paralysed confronted with such helplessness. They need twenty-four-hour watching and they've got no conversation.

NINOTCHKA (to Babushka). Liar!

BABUSHKA (to Ninotchka). I am just not at one with the children of this world. They make me feel childish!

NINOTCHKA. Liar!

BABUSHKA. And this is not the world I want to bring them into.

NINOTCHKA. Liar!

BABUSHKA. Your whole life has to revolve round them.

NINOTCHKA. Liar! Liar!

BABUSHKA. All right! I'm too busy, too young, too selfish. I want my body firm, I want it to stay the way it is. I can't bear pain, change, time passing, disappointment, all that loving, all that doting, all that dependency, giving, giving, giving! What can I do? I'm just not maternal. Some people are born tone-deaf, dyslexic, brain-damaged, they have deficiencies, allergies – I once had a client who was allergic to herself – what can I do? I don't have the imagination to comprehend what it's like to be a child and not to be an adult. Jesus Christ!

Back up to behind the cutting-table.

SAMANTHA. I came up here to work not to be stretched on the rack by the Inquisition. Why am I letting this woman upset me? And why isn't it time for the phone to ring?

NINOTCHKA (*angrily pressing Babushka*). And will you destroy for him? And will you betray who you are for him? And will you offend what you value for him? And cripple and mock and pollute and spit upon all that you love for him?

BABUSHKA. Yes! Yes! Yes! Haven't you heard? There is a curse upon the land. The best men have been turned to stone. There is a dearth of poets. I'll never find another like him!

Exhausted. On the verge of tears.

She sits on the edge of rostrum between her 'girls'. Unpins her hair loose.

Oh, I ache to be young again. I miss, I miss, I so miss my days of blood and youth.

NINOTCHKA. Cursi, Babushka, cursi, cursi, cursi!

BABUSHKA. *Not* cursi. Pain is not cursi.

NINOTCHKA. But nostalgia is.

JESSICA. What do you think a psychiatrist would get out of her if not nostalgia? Talk, Samantha, tell us about your youth.

NINOTCHKA. Especially the 'bloody' part.

JESSICA. Ignore her, Sam. She's an acerbic old hag. We've all got one of those for a friend. Come. Youth. Parents. Mother and father. Start with them.

★ ★ ★

Now we really witness a tortured soul wrestling with itself.

BABUSHKA. They had a great capacity for joy.

NINOTCHKA. You realise power goes from you to him, Babushka. . . ?

BABUSHKA. They could dance disco in the middle of the day.

NINOTCHKA. . . . that he will still set the ground-rules, your balanced man?

BABUSHKA. Come the spring they'd rush out each morning to see which flowers were breaking through.

NINOTCHKA. You can't confide in anyone . . .

BABUSHKA. They delighted in their children, their grandchildren, good food, good wine, other people's success.

NINOTCHKA. . . . and the odd night is never enough . . .

BABUSHKA. It was their nature to be happy as the nature of some was to be joyless . . .

NINOTCHKA. . . . and there's no real equality . . .

BABUSHKA. . . . to be generous as others were mean . . .

NINOTCHKA. . . . no genuine give and take . . .

BABUSHKA. . . . sunny as others were sour . . .

NINOTCHKA. . . . no real future.

BABUSHKA. . . . they had angers, frailties, flaws but – I don't know – one felt happier when they were around. They had a still centre. The parts held . . .

NINOTCHKA. Face it, Babushka. This affair is demeaning and lonely.

BABUSHKA. . . . the parts held. They radiated. We basked in it. Stretched our limbs and depended upon it.

NINOTCHKA. And there is still the one big blinding question to be answered isn't there?

BABUSHKA. And they attracted hatred and they attracted devotion and we adored them and I miss them, I miss them, I miss them.

SAMANTHA (*lullaby*). Sam, Sam, Babushka's Sam.

She turns back to her ironing and speaks fast as though to drown out the other voices.

And he has all these weird and wonderful ideas for making a fortune. To be made for life! Always looking to be made for life. He wants to rent out farmland to African states which suffer from drought. He wants to write a history of revolutions which massacre their thinkers and burn their books. He has this idea for a new diet of citrus fruits and honey in the morning and yoghurt and honey in the evening and it's very good I've tried it but I'll never be any good at diets I'm too curious to be disciplined or moral about anything.

Abrupt halt.

Returns skirt to rack. To desk. Looks at sheaf of appeals.

'The National Jazz Centre, a fund-raising concert . . .'
'Committee to Defend South Korean Socialists . . .'
'Oxfam . . .'

'Dear Miss Milner . . . our productions will integrate the different parts of performance disciplines . . . dance, movement, mime, acting . . . our first production . . . *Petrushka* . . . in the piazza of Covent Garden . . .'

My dresses probably end up in Oxfam shops, and South Korean Socialists have lots of comrades . . .

> *Sits. Reaches for cheque book.*

No one is supporting jazz or the arts . . . (*Writing.*) Project *Petrushka* . . . one hundred pounds . . . National Jazz Centre . . . one hundred pounds . . .

NINOTCHKA. I think guilts are cursi, Babushka. Cursyonomy of the heart. There! (*Swivelling round to her.*) I've coined a new word. Cursyonomy. Cursyonomous. Cursionic. Cursyisms.

> *She 'rides' her chair round and round.*

Throw everything at them – old age, physical handicap, starvation! Give them no rest! Afflicted children, cultural neglect, plundering capitalists! Agitate them! Distress them! Interfere with their happiness! Maimed animals, oppression, deprivation, disease, disaster! Cursi! Cursi! Cursi, cursi, cursi!

> *Confronts phone.*

The phone's out of order! He's had an accident! His wife's had an accident! One of his children! God in heaven, it's time! Ring, damn you! Rescue me. (*Looking at letters.*) I – NEED – RESCUING!

'If we are honest,' it will begin, 'all things must end . . .'

* * *

NINOTCHKA. And what will you do then, Babushka?

Rage? (*Rising to her.*) Let me tell you about rage. Like a wife you'll rage. You could find words to justify his betrayal for *you*. (*Mock ardour.*) 'Where is your courage, adventure, your manhood? Can't you see that to love me is the risk of thrilling risks? How can you deny such a grand passion?' Oh yes, Babushka, you had the language to taunt, inflame and justify loving your 'man with the still centre'. But for *him* to leave *you*? For *him* to betray *you*? You have hell in you ready for that, have you not, Babushka? Oh have you not! Queen of the double-standard. That's you! Of the double-standard, queen!

BABUSHKA. Stop her, Jessica, stop her or I'll do something drastic.

NINOTCHKA. And the question, Babushka, the one big blinding question? Are you ready for it? All that lovely honesty set up to receive it? Think you've given enough away to charity?

JESSICA. Too far, Ninotchka, too far! You don't really care about honesty, do you? All you care about is pain. You're jealous aren't you? You don't think she deserves what she's achieved, do you? It's not fair to be endowed with beauty *and* talent *and* good fortune *and* a lovely loving lover. What a mean and tawdry little tart you are, Ninotchka. What an ungenerous, tight-arsed, sanctimonious vixen, a killer, a sadistic despot, a . . .

NINOTCHKA. Ask her! Ask her! Let's have none of your pious mercy, Jessica. No lachrymosity this night, my friend. This night is judgement night. Ask her:

How can she *love* a man who betrays his wife? Ask her that?

SAMANTHA. Get-her-out-of-my-head-please-phone-me-eeeeeee!

Suddenly seeing hot iron near her she grabs it on to her hand.

Screams.

Reaches for water-dispenser under her ironing-table. Sprays her hand.

JESSICA. You've been drinking too much, Sam.

SAMANTHA. I know I have, Jessica, I know it.

JESSICA. Stop working, stop drinking, stop talking to yourself.

Moves to desk. Finds cloth in a drawer to wrap round her hand.

SAMANTHA. Yes, Jessica, I will, I will. I'll do all that.

JESSICA. You can have a chocolate or two but not the liqueurs. I don't know why you've worked yourself up into such a state tonight, Sam. Why tonight of all nights? 'Wherefore is this night different from all other nights?'

Long, long pause as she considers this question.

(*Lullaby.*) Sam, Sam, Babushka's Sam . . .

Picks up sheaf of appeals.

Lights fade very, very slowly.

'Amnesty International . . .'
'Jews Against Ethnic Cleansing . . .'
'Christian Aid . . .'
'Dear Samantha Milner, to you the suffering in the world may seem never-ending. Horrors that cry out for help. Your help. And sometimes you almost wish you could forget. Until . . .'

Blackout.

Letter to a Daughter

*A play in six parts with songs
for an actress who can sing*

Letter to a Daughter was first performed by the Sanwoo-lim Theatre Company, Seoul, Korea, on 20 March 1992, with Suk-Hwa Yoon, directed by Young-Woong Lim, designed by Dongwoo Park, with music composed by Dong-Jin Cho.

I am grateful to Professor Duk-Ae Chung of Seoul University, who heard me read this play to the British Council's International Cambridge Seminar in 1991, translated it immediately and proposed it to the director of the Sanwoolim Theatre Company.

Letter to a Daughter was first performed in the UK on 8 August 1998 in the Observer Assembly Rooms during the Edinburgh Festival, with Julie Clare, directed by Arnold Wesker, designed by Eric Rehl, with music composed by Benjamin Till.

Originally composition of the music was open to an indigenous composer. After the Edinburgh Festival it is hoped that Ben Till's music will be used.

PART ONE

MELANIE, *a singer/composer of ballads. Aged thirty-five.*

In the darkness we hear her voice in song.

Lights up on her studio/workroom.

She is surrounded by recording and playback equipment and all her comforts including:

- *an espresso coffee machine for two*
- *a huge soft armchair in which she seems to live*
- *a music lectern on which her score rests*
- *and a desk on which lie the sheets of the letter she's writing to her daughter.*

Her space is vibrant with pot-plants.

She is dressed in an old flowered silk dressing gown. Flowing. Theatrical. Dramatic.

She is dramatic. Perhaps energetic is a better description – strong, energetic, restless, unpredictable.

Four actions occupy MELANIE *throughout the play:*

- *watering her plants*
- *fixing a fuse when the lights go out*
- *completing, on the floor, a photomontage of her daughter*
- *and slowly making up, preparing for 'an event'.*

Prominent is a telephone answering-machine.

The answering-machine and the photomontage are the 'other people' in the room to whom she speaks.

Six songs will punctuate the six parts of the play.

We find her rehearsing the last verse of a song she has just written.

MELANIE.

> No one can take
> From our time
> No one can shake
> The halcyon memories
> When nothing was beyond
> Our hopeful energies
> And every day
> In every way
> Was our time.

Not bad. Not good but not bad. Perhaps good but not great.

> *Writes corrections on her score.*

What's 'great' anyway? Who knows what's 'great' until long afterwards. Time makes things 'great'.

> *Re-thinks that.*

Not true! You're sensitive? You *know* what's great.

> *Re-thinks that, too.*

Not true! *I* know sensitive people who got it wrong. Sensitive, intelligent, knowledgeable – wrong! Should have known better – wrong! I've sung them new songs they should have recognised at once – wrong! And it's understandable – if they were right all the time they'd be rich. (*Beat.*) Some of them *are* rich!

Ah, Melanie, Melanie, Melanie! If you can't work it out for yourself how can you work it out for your daughter?

> *She moves to her desk to look at a sheet on which she has been writing.*

'My dear daughter, there comes a time in a young woman's life –'

Shit! That's a dreadful start.

Sits at her desk to start again.

(*Writing.*) 'Daughter mine. Some things are difficult to talk about and so I've decided to try and write you a letter instead . . .'

Stares at the sheet a long time.

As though writing was easier than talking! Just because you're not looking her in the eye doesn't mean the words come more easily. Matching words to thoughts is difficult whether someone's in front of you or not. It's thinking that's difficult – not finding the right words. *What* to say *that's* what's hard.

Sits on back of armchair to continue writing.

'Dear Marike, the problem is – young women have problems!'

Considers.

Did I *really* write that? (*Self-mocking.*) '. . . the problem is – young women have problems!' Cretin! Of course young women have problems. She knows young women have problems! She's a young woman with problems! In fact because she's smart, your daughter, she also knows *old* women have problems. (*In one breath.*) Like her mother who isn't old she's only thirty-five but when you're eleven anything over sixteen is old and twenty is middle-aged and thirty is ancient and if you make it to thirty-five it's surprising to them you're still alive!

Looks down at her sheet again.

(*Contemptuously.*) 'Young women have problems!' Who *hasn't* got problems? Everyone's got problems! Young, old, rich, poor, the wise, the foolish, the beautiful, the ugly, the brave, the cowardly! No! Not the cowardly.

The *coward* has no problems. He runs. Takes no risks. No risks – no problems.

Glances at her sheet.

'Young women have problems!' Oh boy, Melanie, what a pain in the arse you are. Mother? Millstone round her neck more like! Nothing to hand on! Stupid as shit!

She lets out a cry of frustration that builds and explodes –

'Dear Marike – your tits are growing!'

That arrests her. Makes her smile. Perhaps that's the way to begin.

'Dear Marike – your tits are growing. You told me so. "Don't touch me, Mother," you said, "I feel very tender there."'

Satisfied.

Good! Revealed in one! No pussyfooting! Straight to the point! That's the way everything should be.

Re-thinks that.

Not true! Sometimes it's cleverer to be devious. Sometimes it's even polite to be devious. Even amusing!

But – ?

But not this time.

'Dear Marike, your tits are growing. You told me so. "Don't touch me, Mother," you said, "I feel very tender there."

From here on she has no need to keep 'writing'. The letter will be constructed in her head.

'Well, I won't touch you there but take it from me – the

tenderness will go. You'll get used to them. Soon you won't be able to *stop* touching them. You'll want *every*one to be touching them!'

She performs a little 'scene' of the young girl who is trying to combine modesty with bravado, coy one minute, bold the next, retiring then – thrusting.

Wait! Who am I writing to? My daughter aged eleven? My daughter aged fourteen? Sixteen? Twenty-one?

But something else troubles her. She moves, as if drawn, to the tape recorder. Presses 'on'.

MAN'S VOICE. Hi, Melanie – at least I hope it's Melanie. I know, I know, you haven't heard from me in a long time and here I am not even in person but on a sodding answer-machine . . .

Switches 'off'.

MELANIE. At twenty-one it's too late. A man could have destroyed her for life by twenty-one.

Really?

Let's not be sexist about it – she could have destroyed her life with*out* anybody's help by twenty-one! Sixteen? If she hasn't got a mother's advice by sixteen she could be pregnant. Fourteen? (*Considers.*) Fourteen! A letter to my daughter aged fourteen.

She reaches for a watering gun.

So – (*Continuing letter in her head.*) 'Soon you'll want everyone to be touching them. I can remember when I first saw mine growing. Sat in front of the mirror for hours, day after day, closing my eyes, covering them with my hands to feel if they were more of a handful, weighing them like melons.'

A mischievous thought –

I wonder if boys do the same thing.

> *She looks down between her legs. Stretches her arms as though pulling out a tape measure, measures 'it'.*

'Dear son. Your "ahem" is growing. You told me so. "Don't touch me there it's tender . . ."'

No! No! Not possible! Thank God I have a daughter. What on earth do you *say* to boys? They don't understand what you're talking about until they're thirty, anyway!

MAN'S VOICE. Hi, Melanie – at least I hope it's Melanie. I know, I know, you haven't heard from me in a long time and here I am not even in person but on a sodding answer-machine . . .

> *Her lights flicker.*

MELANIE. Fix the plug, you'll end up in flames.

'And then came the day I had to buy my first bra. I was so excited. A light blue check thing it was. Really pretty, I thought. Long before I understood lace. And I looked myself in the eye, very serious, very dramatic, as though God had given me the world to look after, and I said: you – are a woman.'

SONG ONE

Said woman, said child no more

Said woman
Said child no more
Said woman, said growing
Said change
And winds blowing
Away innocent confusions
Of day after day
Not knowing if I was coming or going
Said woman
Said child no more.

Said woman
Said child no more
Said all things are changing
Rearranging themselves
Softly thawing themselves into meaning and
   place
Said woman discover
And relish life cherish life as a lover
Said woman
Said child no more.

Little did I know that life shapes you away from
   your dreams
Little did I know how the wanton world weans
   you
On passions beyond your control and means you
For other things than spring's dewy dreams for
   you.

Little did I know we were all born with shadows
Little did I know each one has her terrors

Of failure, rejection, this world too large a place
For one woman's arms to protect and embrace.

Said woman
Said child no more
Said woman love yourself, love
Yourself
There's wealth
For you
In this rich world waiting
To nurture you
Happy and healthy, glowing and wealthy
Said woman
Said child no more.

Said woman
Said child no more
Said no more sugar and spice
Said all
The worthwhile loves
Land in your hand with a tag-price
Which you have to pay
Sooner or later
So learn never to make the same mistake twice
Be woman
Be child no more, no more.

Said woman
Said child no more
Said woman, said growing
Said change
And winds blowing
Away innocent confusions
Of day after day
Not knowing if I was coming or going
Said woman
Said child no more
Said woman

Said child no more
Said woman
Said child no more
Said woman, said child
Said woman, said child
Said woman
Said child no more.

PART TWO

'Why do I want to write this letter at all? Why don't I wait for you to ask me *questions*? So much advice is useless advice, as we all know to our cost. How do I know what it is you'll *want* to know or *need* to know in three years' time when you're fourteen?'

MAN'S VOICE. Hi, Melanie – at least I hope it's Melanie. I know, I know, you haven't heard from me in a long time and here I am not even in person but on a sodding answer-machine . . .

MELANIE. Perhaps it's not a letter to Marike aged fourteen but to Melanie aged thirty-five.

Dear Melanie, you are thirty-five years old. Your life is a mess. How did this come about?

Good! Revealed in one. No pussyfooting. Straight to the point! That's the way everything should be.

Not true. That's *not* the point. It's not that your life is a mess it's that you're tired of who you are and you want to be someone else and you don't know if you've got it in you to change.

> *Pause.*

Or if you've got anything inside you to change to!

Not true! Your life *is* a mess. It's a mess and you've got this major decision to make, and it's tearing you apart, and . . . and . . . Stop talking about your*self*. God! You're such a self-centred prima donna! You're supposed to be giving this time to your daughter and her tender tits!

'My dear Marike, I have things I want to tell you. Not

to be read now but when you're fourteen. You are a woman and everyone will tell you that being a woman is hell and ecstasy but here's the first and most important thing *I* have to tell you: it's hell and ecstasy for everyone! Mostly hell. So no self-pity, no favours, no special pleading. Except this: when God shared out ecstasy he decided men should have more than women, so he gave women to men and gave us men. (*Beat.*) Mostly! (*Beat.*) Don't ask me why; in fact "why" is not something you should ever ask.

Re-thinks that.

'Not true! You should *always* ask. Why? Why, why, why?

Re-thinks that, too.

'But not for everything. Why is the sky blue? Yes – the answer could be interesting. Why are people stupid? No point – it's a fact of life. Why did I do such and such? Yes – the answer could be useful for next time. Why is water wet? No point – it's wet! Starving people die, fire burns, fish can't fly – fact. *Why* are people starving – *that* you can ask. And *who* set fire to the house – *that* you can ask. And why pain, why anger, why does he love me, why does he hate me, why did he leave me? But fire always burns, water is always wet, and fish will never fly.'

Surprised, but pleased with herself.

That's quite good.

To the answer-machine.

Perhaps I'm not as stupid as shit after all!

MAN'S VOICE. Hi, Melanie – at least I hope it's Melanie. I know, I know, you haven't heard from me in a long time and here I am not even in person but on a sodding answer-machine . . . Well, I thought my voice would sound better than my pen. No personality in a pen is there? Easier to lie with ink than with the old vocal cords. And you could always *tell* when I was lying. But I'm not lying now . . . You see . . . what I want . . . what I'm asking . . . what I'd like, what I'd *really* like . . . I *know* what I did, I know a lot of years have passed but – Shit! What made me think it'd be easier on a sodding answer-machine. . . ?

> *Pretends she's heard nothing – like ignoring someone who's in the room. The lights flicker again.*

MELANIE. The wires are loose! Fix the bloody loose wiring!

> *But she doesn't. Returns to montage.*

'Now my dear daughter, here's the good news. You *wanted* to come into this world. Absolutely no doubt. The odds were against you but you fought like mad. How do I know? Here's the bad news – you shouldn't have happened. I wore a coil, made love, and fell pregnant. The coil was supposed to give me freedom. And the doctor warned me: because of the coil you may lose your baby. Never! Nothing was going to stop you. "I'm coming!" you yelled. "It's my time!" and you burst through, screaming fit to bring down the walls of Jericho.'

> *Again the memory of the message returns, as though from another person in the room by whom she feels threatened.*

MAN'S VOICE. . . . I hope you're still listening, and if you are I'll come straight to the point – I know how you always hate pussyfooting about. 'No pussyfooting about' you used to say, 'straight to the point! The way everything should be!' Remember? Used to make me smile. And you smiled, too. (*Beat.*) When I was around. (*Beat.*) But I wasn't around much was I? (*Pause.*) I'm pussyfooting about aren't I? (*Beat.*) But I want to be. (*Beat.*) Around that is. (*Beat.*) With my daughter. (*Beat.*) Watch her grow and . . .

> *Memories return. She doesn't want them. Needs to make them go.*

MELANIE. 'And how I loved carrying you. Once *I* knew you were inside me I wanted *every*one to know, to see how capable I could be, how responsible I was. I couldn't swell fast enough. When my belly was still flat I used to arch my back and pretend you were just a few weeks away instead of eight months. As soon as the doctor told me you were coming I rushed out and bought smocks and flat sensible shoes. I was going to do everything right for you. Whatever the textbook ordered – I was going to obey.

> *Her mood changes.*

'And did I, Marike? Go on, ask me. Did I?

> *She has a facility for talking herself up and down, into and out of moods.*

'Did I, hell! Nothing I hated more than flat, sensible shoes. No man would ever look at me again, I thought. And those smocks! Probably the unsexiest things ever conceived – except for Bermuda shorts – and your mother was not going to be caught being un-sexy! Being sexy was very important to your mother, it was what your mother imagined earned her a *place* in the world; not brains or personality or achievement but a firm bum, erect nipples, wet lips, flashing eyes, and sultry glances – a body moving healthily through the streets and glowing with promise. So it was high heels and tight skirts in no time at all! I'm telling you – I carried you around in my belly for nine months and fed my brains on fears of rejection. Developed a head like jelly, went berserk at weekends, became a weekend hippie, smoked grass, imagined I was living a glamorous life. But I hated grass. And I felt guilty. You've got this child in your womb I yelled at myself. Grass can destroy its brain cells, give you cancer, create hormone changes! Then I'd argue with myself. Shit! It's only grass! Everyone smokes grass! I haven't seen anyone die of grass. Smoked! Drank! Danced! Opened my legs and humped up and down but nothing, nothing stopped you rocketing out of my abused body screaming! Screaming, flailing your arms, fisting everything in sight! Whoosh! Demanding life! Whoosh! Grabbing at the air with greedy hands – lungs like bellows. Whoosh!

'And here's the second and most important thing I have to tell you: firm bum, wet lips and sultry glances bring down upon you the idiot male population – all hands, hot breath and monosyllabic conversation. Grab knowledge! Wear tight skirts but grab knowledge! Let your nipples stand erect but grab knowledge! You grabbed air to breathe, now grab knowledge to defend yourself in this God-almighty rotten world. Whooosh!

'But not everything was right, and here's the third and most important thing I've got to tell you. It's so important that perhaps it should have been the first and most important thing I told you:

> *To the answer-machine, 'him', who now becomes a second presence in the room.*

everything you do has a consequence. Not necessarily bad, but as sure as night follows day follows night follows day – consequences follow actions. That's what it means to be thoughtful: to consider consequences.

To Marike.

'I didn't. Your father fled, I lived wild, and you came out sick – screaming with life but half dead, and you had to go straight into an incubator. For a long time. And I cried. Boy! Did I cry. And to recompense you I swore I'd breast-feed you – and I did.

Drifts into memory.

'And sang you to sleep with lullabies.'

SONG TWO

Lullaby – Kisses and cream

I will give her kisses and the cream off the milk
And pull down the clouds to warm her ears
She will touch my lips with a tongue of silk
And sing away my tears.

Do not make me weep with that look in your
    eyes
And I will give you honey, little girl, and a bear
You can pester me with all of your 'whys'
There'll be sunlight through the year.

She will give me cuddles and sleepless nights
And moan with her long growing pains
What will she dream of these first nights?
She will call me her own name.

I will give her kisses and the cream of my time
And a penny to buy black sweets
And her wide laugh will last longer than mine
As she grows in the streets.

I will give you kisses and the cream off the milk
And reasons why you were born, why you were
    born
And I will feel the touch of her tongue of silk
Long, long after her youth is gone.

PART THREE

'Not true! I *never* sang you lullabies.'

She is in a distressed state.

What the hell am I writing this letter for? What do *I* have to tell my daughter that could possibly be of any use to her? I'm trying to unravel the mess I made of *my* life, what use can *that* be to her?

On the other hand –

Who says you have to be perfect to give advice? Who's perfect?

Long pause.

'Your father wants to be part of your life. (*Beat.*) After eleven years.

Pause.

'You asked about him and I told you some things but – not everything. He's a musician, I told you. In great demand, I told you. Had to be here, there and everywhere, I told you. So *he* decided – unilaterally – learn that word, I had to, means you make decisions without consulting anyone else – unilaterally he decided: it was unfair to give you a father who'd never be there, so – he left the moment he knew you were coming. (*Beat.*) Left us free to find a better one. That's what I told you. Made him a kind of hero. Self-sacrificing. Noble.

'Truth is – he was the coward who ran. (*Beat.*) And I could find no one.

Pause. Shakes herself out of it.

'No, I never sang you lullabies. But I did have dreams for you. Before you were born of course. Four months old inside me and I was plotting complete lifetimes – from the cradle to the grave. And of course in each one you were famous. My daughter? Had to be!

'Actress! Surgeon! Astronaut! Ballet dancer! Poet! Crazy! I was a crazy pregnant mother, crippling your life with decisions even before you were born. Crazy!

Going easier on herself.

'On the other hand is it such a *bad* thing to have ambitions for your child? My problem was *no* one had ambitions for me.

Recalls this, sadly.

'Oh, my parents loved me. At least my daddy did. Only he never told me until after he'd had three glasses of wine, and then his eyes announced he adored me. Used to upset my mother. She could see emotions in his face that *she* could never arouse. He adored me, was tender, protective and it all used to upset her and I never understood why.

'Here's a story for you. I was about twelve – my father said to me "Right, let's see if you're afraid of the dark." And he took me by the hand and he led me to the cellar and he put me inside and he locked the door. And there I stood. For long, long minutes. Just me and the silence. No fear. No panic. No emotion. Just – what next I thought? And then I heard my father's voice: "Well Melanie? Are you afraid of the dark?" And I replied: "I don't know, Daddy. I can't see anything!"

'He loved that. Oh how he loved that. Made him laugh! Laugh and laugh and laugh and laugh. Couldn't stop telling the story to his friends and neighbours. And every time he told it he laughed as though he was telling it for the first time. And the story grew. "I took Melanie down to the cellar and it was full of spiders . . ." Then it was full of rats! Then he switched the light on and off. Then he made ghostly sounds. ". . . I left her for three minutes . . . for thirty minutes . . . for an hour. . . !" And he laughed! He had the kind of laughter made you want to laugh with him. Infectious. Bold. And I loved him. He was a father who didn't want his daughter to be afraid of anything. We went to the sea once and there was a huge storm and he stood with me in front of these big waves which were crashing towards us making the most frightening noise ever and he shouted above it ". . . Don't be afraid of the elements . . . never be afraid of the elements. You hear those waves? Shout back at them, shout back, shout back . . ."

She's shouting. Stops. Surprised. Collects herself.

'But he had no ambitions for me. He used to say: "I don't care if you drive a taxi as long as you're happy doing it." No ambition for me.

It saddens her to remember. But she revives.

'So at seventeen I quit school without taking my exams and joined an academy to learn how to teach music to children. Three years. And that seemed all right to my daddy. Nothing wrong with that. Nothing special but – OK! – A schoolteacher! Humble teachers sometimes taught children who became great men and women . . .

Mind drifts –

'Just didn't give *me* much of a buzz though. I like children but –

drift . . . drift . . .

'My daddy – your grandfather.

drift . . .

'I'm sorry you never saw him.

drift . . .

'Your grandfather – my daddy.

drift . . .

'If someone laughed at him I used to cry. Cry. I used to cry if someone laughed at him.

drift . . .

'Drank too much!

drift . . . *drift* . . .

'No. I never sang you lullabies.

Shakes herself alert.

'Didn't play with you much, either. Or invent stories. Imagine! I trained as a music teacher for children and I used to make up stories and invent complicated musical games for them – but never for you! Invented nothing with my own daughter! And when I did do the things mothers should do – like knitting, making dresses, teaching you how to read – I didn't always succeed. I confess – I loved the idea of having a child of my own but I wasn't what you'd call a "natural" mother. Didn't come to me easily. In fact many would say it didn't come to me at all.

To 'him'.

'But at least I was *there*. Getting it wrong but – *there*! *I* didn't run.

To Marike.

'And I used to touch you a lot. It was the time everyone was touching. Be tactile! everyone used to say. If you touched someone it was a sign you cared for them. But

I wonder. Depends who's doing the touching. *I* was touched. The boys couldn't *stop* touching me, but I can't remember any of them really *caring* for me. Not in our crowd. My "peers"!

'And here's the fourth and most important thing I have to tell you: select your peers. In fact it might be the only *most* important thing I have to tell you because if you get this wrong then anything else I tell you will go down the drain.

'Select your peers. Don't go with the herd. Don't look to be one of the gang. I know there's great comfort in a gang, in belonging, in being accepted but – resist it! A gang consists of people who are living their lives *through* each other. Ask me – I know! I was part of a gang, one of the girls, always busy being what I thought would please the others, picking up their bad habits, thinking their thoughts, sharing their stupid prejudices, laughing at their mindless hatreds. We never questioned each other, we just stroked each other's nonsense. "Right!" we'd say. "You've said it! Good for you! You've hit the nail on the head." We *thought* we were strong but we were all terrified of stepping out of line. Not one of us was independent. Not one of us had an opinion that was our own. And we intimidated each other. If one of us dared to say "I don't agree! I don't think we should", out would come that dreary old cry: "Who does she think she is? Who *does* she *think* she *is*!"

'I think I hated that cry more than any other in the whole wide world. If anyone cries it out to you, Marike, you tell them: she thinks she's an individual! She thinks she can think her own thoughts! She thinks she can rise above the herd! You tell them that.

Panic.

'No! Don't! They'll slaughter you! What advice am I

giving you, for God's sake! This is a crazy letter. You have a "crazy" for a mother. Don't, whatever you do, don't stand above the herd. In fact don't even think of them as the herd. They are *not* a herd, a herd is cattle, dumb animals. They're not dumb animals. They're your (*Sardonically.*) brothers and sisters, your comrades-in-arms, your link to reality, your support system. Stay with them for God's sake or they'll tear you limb from limb.

Panic turns to defiance.

'Then take the risk! Stand out! *Fly* . . .'

SONG THREE

Fly

Fly from their reach
Fly from their reach
Beware of befriending
Those not worth defending
Hold youth's magic dance
Please do not lose
Youth's magic dance
Fly!
You're given one chance
Only one chance.

Fly from their frost
Fly fly from their frost
The cost of remaining
With their stale complaining
Is youth's magic dance
Please do not lose
Youth's magic dance
Fly!
You're given one chance
Only one chance.

Cry 'My time to dance
My time, my time to dance
Oh, I'm given one chance
Only one chance.'

Fly from their taunts
Fly fly fly from their taunts
What haunts is confusion
Their pain, their disillusion
Hold youth's magic dance

Please do not lose
Youth's magic dance
Fly
You're given one chance
Only one chance.

Cry 'My time to dance
My time, my time to dance
Oh, I'm given one chance
Only one chance.'

I'd take your pains
I'd weep your tears
I'd bear your shame
And all your poor mistakes make mine
This cannot be.
And so prepare
For what I cannot do for you
For that I cannot die for you
Though I would do and die for you
Prepare
You must do all for you.

Cry 'My time to dance
My time, my time to dance
Oh, I'm given one chance
Only one chance.'
Oh, cry 'My time to dance
My time to dance
Oh, I'm given one chance
Yes, I'm given one chance
Only one chance.'

PART FOUR

(*Pointing to answer-machine.*) Shall we let him into your life, Marike? A man you've never known? He used to come home smelling of booze and bigotry. (*Imitating.*) 'Foreigners! Foreigners! Too many fucking foreigners!' He was a moron and he brought morons into the house. Morons and loud-mouthed clods. Had a weakness for idiots. Do you need such a father?

The lights go out.

Shit! Shit shit shit!

She rummages around in the dark.

Matches! Where are the fucking matches?

Finds them. Lights three candles.

See what happens if you leave undone things undone? The light goes! You become blind! I should have seen to those loose wires months ago.

The fuse. Need to change the fuse.

Reaches for plug, lays it on armchair.

Screwdriver. Where's the sodding screwdriver?

Looks for and finds screwdriver.

I hate messing with electricity. It's a phobia. Some people have a phobia about heights, some people have a phobia about crowds, I have a phobia about fish bones and electricity.

Extracts old fuse. Regards it.

You haven't got a new fuse, have you?

And here's something else I have to tell you, Marike, which is just as important as anything I *have* told you or am *likely* to tell you: don't put off until tomorrow what should be done today! Because if you do it today and enjoy it you can do it again tomorrow!

Has amused herself.

No no, let's be serious. I'm your mother. Being frivolous is not allowed. Procrastinate and the lights go out!

On the other hand *candle*light is romantic.

Fuse! Concentrate on the fuse.

She has to extract fuse from hi-fi plug.

Grrrrr! I hate such fiddly things. Times like this I know why I need a man!

OK, daughter – pros and cons. He might have changed – pro! He might be worse – con! He'll love you – pro! I'll hate him – con! He blew a good trumpet – and oh, could he blow – pro! But he blew hot and cold – con. Fathers are relaxed about life, they balance tense mothers – pro! Tense mothers are useful, they sense dangers – con! Fathers hand on courage – pro! Con – not this one. He'll hand on dogma, intolerance and beery hatred. The original ethnic cleanser.

Pro – life softens the edges. Con – she'll see I despise him. Does it matter? If your daughter's made happy do *your* feelings matter? How could she be happy with a father who abandoned her? Children forgive – pro! Are *you* so clever you can criticise him – pro. She's going to look for him one day – pro. And pro – what kind of a life did you give her anyway?

Long pause. She's now competing with him for her daughter even though he's not there!

'My dear Marike, let me tell you something I've always wanted to tell you about yourself. You know your most dangerous quality? You learn too easily. Everything comes to you without much effort and so you don't *make* much effort. Me – I had to work hard to comprehend *any*thing! Nothing came easily! And if there's one thing in my life that I can offer you as an example there's my discipline as a singer. Discipline! I rehearse non-stop. I go over a song again and again, worrying at it, to make it better, to make my voice reach out, to stretch myself. What's there I make work to the utmost.'

(*Wildly declaiming.*) TO –THEEEEEE – UTMOST!

> *At which point she bursts into an energetic but very, very difficult melody that takes her voice up and down between extreme registers.*

> *She looks dramatic singing in the candlelight.*

SONG FOUR

Nothing comes easy

Nothing comes easy
And I'll sing it again and again and again
Worry it, hone it
Trim it, dethrone it
Bring it before you
And try to ignore what you've chosen
Too often you've chosen
What is lifeless and frozen
Your darlings are dead
Get rid of them
Get rid of them
Sing pure. Sing pure
Remembering
Nothing comes easy
Surely nothing comes easy.

Nothing comes easy
Look at the way that I worry all day
High note and low note
Wrong note and right note
Have, have I made it work
Is my talent in tune
With my passion
Will I ruin career
With anxiety, fear
Am I bold enough
Able to stand on a stage
And sing. And sing
Remembering
Nothing comes easy
Oh God, nothing comes easy
Nothing comes easy.

Nothing comes easy
Sing it again and again and again
Look at it, doubt it
Whisper it, shout it
Critics ignore you
Neglect or restore you
Beware of their bile and their praises
Your life and your art
Each is a craft to be worked at
Worked at
Worked hard at, worked hard at
Remembering
Nothing comes easy
But nothing, nothing comes
Nothing comes easy.

High note low note
Wrong note right note
Worry it hone it
Trim it dethrone it
Will I ruin career
With anxiety, fear
Am I bold enough
Able to stand on a stage
And sing. And sing. And sing
Remembering
Nothing
Oh God, nothing comes easy.

PART FIVE

MELANIE, *exhausted, flops into her armchair to continue fixing the wires into the plug.*

'Why, you are asking yourself, is she writing all this to me? OK, so my tits are growing. Big deal! I'll get over it! If I'd known I'd get all these pages of garbage, I'd have kept quiet about my tits growing.

'You're right! But I've got a confession to make. Your growing tits make *me* think about growing up. You're facing change and decisions in *your* life – I'm facing change and decisions in my life.

'You've noticed, haven't you! Of course you've noticed. What else accounts for my short temper, my loud voice, my creeping away for hours on end? Poor Marike. What a lot you've had to put up with these last months from this crazy who creeps around your flat.

'I sit watching television and I think, why are you watching television? Why aren't you doing something for your daughter? So then I feel guilty for neglecting you, for not being a constructive mum, for not shaping your talents, your personality. And I get angry with you for making me feel guilty and suddenly I have *two* reasons for hating myself. And boy! no one can hate me like I hate me! *Every*thing comes back. I've got a memory like a sewer, all the smells of a rotten past rise up and I have to take a shower. You've noticed, I know. Sometimes I have to take a shower three times on a really bad evening and I can see you watching me. Frightened. And I hate frightening you, I really do, honest, just hate it. And it adds to my anger which adds to my guilt which adds to my hate which adds to my anger . . . I try hard to correct myself but I get like a child – I can *see* I'm doing wrong but I don't care. I just do not care!

The plug is fixed.

Lights!

'And oh, did I do a lot of things wrong!

As she speaks she blows out the candles.

'I over-estimated how much you could manage on your own. (*Blow.*) I used to leave you alone to go and do gigs when you were only six years old. Six! I can hardly bring myself to confess it. Six! (*Blow.*) You hear of apartments catching fire and children burnt to death while parents are out for a drink and that could have been you! Christ Almighty! I go cold just thinking about it. (*Blow.*) I was a monster! An irresponsible monster!'

She storms at the answer-machine.

No! Don't you fucking criticise me. You weren't there! And if you had been it would have been worse. Of *course* I always alerted the neighbours. I wasn't *so* irresponsible. And I'd rig up a rope at her bedside with a bell at the end so they could hear it, and they used to report to me how they could hear her brushing her teeth and singing to herself –

Storming eases.

– singing to herself! To herself! Alone!

To Marike.

'I left you alone! Oh God, Marike, forgive me.

Sits in her armchair, back to the 'daughter' she can hardly face. Fights back tears.

'Sometimes of course I took you with me. The guilt got
so heavy I took you on tours with me. But – but –

Struggles to confess –

– you were a burden! I'll say it – you got in my way.
"Where are you going? How long for? When are you
coming back? Who are you going to see? What are you
going to do? Why can't I come. . . ?" You made me feel
like a dog on a chain! I *had* to be free! "I need my
space!" I shouted. "No one is going to hold me back!" I
raged. "This is my one and only life and I'm going to
live it to the full!" Shouted, raged, scolded, and slunk
off saturated with guilt like sweat, leaving you in your
room so that I could be with the others, always
traceable, messages with reception to say where I was,
but – this woman, this young woman with energy and
appetites was not going to miss out on the fun, was not
going to miss out on anything life had to offer and – oh
my God, Marike, terrible things happened, terrible
awful experiences, traumatic, which you'll never forget
and I'll never forget and I will always feel guilty for
them and – oh my God! Once I was drunk, so drunk –

*She can't bear to face the memory – and perhaps we
don't need to hear it spelt out but can guess at it.*

Weeps.

'Relationships? Minefields! Every relationship is a
minefield.'

To 'him'.

And you want to come back after eleven years?

She's desperate to collect herself.

Quick, think of something good. You haven't been *all*
bad in your life, remember something thoughtful that
you've done.

She paces her room frantically searching memory.

(*Fast.*) 'My dear Marike, we used to sing together in the car!' That's it! 'My dear Marike, we used to love to sing together when we drove to my gigs. Loud, clear, in harmony, full of spirits, laughter, joy! Real joy! And you had such a wonderful voice, my darling, you still have, and I wanted you to sing with the local choir but you didn't want that. "I'm happy just to be singing with you, Mamma. Just us!" And I listened to you. I respected your wishes. You had such large wise eyes when you were a child, I felt . . . I felt . . . what did I feel? I felt I wanted to give you responsibility. That's it! Wanted you to grow strong, to become independent, self-reliant. *That's* why I left you alone because –

Struggling –

'Not true. NOT TRUE! Oh, Christ! I must have done *some*thing right because *you* take care of *me* now. You do, and I love you for doing it. "Mother, you'll be late for your appointment . . . Don't forget the milk . . . You've got a ladder in your stocking . . . The keys, Mother, you've forgotten the keys." Oh, Marike –'

SONG FIVE

Child like you

A child like you is a gift
I didn't recognise the gift
Till now
I didn't learn
I didn't earn the gift
Till now
And now I count the cost
Pray not everything is lost
Carry a heart tossed
With guilt
Mea culpa – guilt
Mea culpa – guilt
Child like you.

Everything I did was wrong
Even when I did it right it was wrong
Can we ever get it right
As love is such a strong
Emotion?

Mother like me can't be bad
I can't be just accused of bad
Take stock
You mustn't kill
You mustn't will away
Your rock
I am your rock, hold fast
I'm all you've got to last
A lifetime till the past
Fades grey
Mea culpa – guilt
Mea culpa – guilt
Child like you.

Fade my anger, fade my guilt
Guilt and anger from your life
Living means you must forgive
Giving love you learn to live and forgive
We cannot both despise and thrive
On lives of rich and strong
Emotion.

A child like you is a gift
I didn't recognise the gift
Till now
I didn't learn
I didn't earn the gift
Till now
And now I count the cost
Pray not everything is lost
Carry a heart tossed
With guilt
A child like you
Oh, *mea culpa* – guilt
Mea culpa – guilt
Mea culpa – guilt
Child like you.

PART SIX

MELANIE *makes herself two espresso coffees in her little Gaggia machine.*

Big, big question: is being a moronic father reason enough to be kept away from the daughter? He's not a violent moron, not a vicious, abusive moron. Just a moron. Can moronic fathers damage their children's health? Would she become like him? (*Beat.*) She could become like me.

Pause.

God! I hope she's not like me.

'Dear daughter, Marike, do-not-be-like-me.

'"What is it to be like you, Mother?"

'Shoot first ask questions later, that's me. Not the way to live.'

Not true! The *only* way to live. To feel. *Feel.* I sometimes think I'll never feel again, that I'll turn to dust before the Grim Reaper hauls me away for good. Who wants to be a dead thing before they're dead?

Pause.

'But, daughter, I'm working at it. Thinking comes hard but I'm working at it. I'm trying to, how shall I put it? I'm trying to – reborn myself. How do you like that? Reborn myself.'

To 'him'.

REBORN MYSELF!

Pause.

The problem is – is it too late? Am I the prisoner of myself?

Appalled.

Now that would be terrifying. That would really be a nightmare to think that at thirty-five I had made my life, my habits, my attitudes, my expectations – a prison. Inescapable. On a train that would never stop and I couldn't jump off and it was all, all, all, too late.

Shakes the terror from herself.

I can't believe that. I mustn't believe that. I refuse to believe that.

'My dear Marike, and here's the fifth and most important thing I have to tell you: beware of emotions. Be emotional if you must but be aware of them. Emotions seduce. I fell deeply in love with myself being full of feeling. One of the easiest things in life is to intoxicate yourself with your favourite image of yourself, and the image of myself that I fell in love with – because *I* thought it made *me* the most interesting, fascinating, deepest of deep creatures in the world – was the image of a magnificently erupting volcano. And friends around encouraged me – they enjoyed the fire, the sparks. Very colourful! Very dramatic!

'As you very well know – your mother was born with this enormous energy, I don't exactly fade into the wallpaper. But, my dear Marike, energy is a woman with two faces: one is violent and can destroy, the other is tender and can nourish. My energy was violent. It destroyed. Five times a year I'd go berserk, crazy, off the rails! And I'd show myself to the world as the arsehole I really am not, believe me! Drink, quarrels, betrayals! I'd break promises, turn up late, freak out in the middle of a gig. No one could depend on me. I was wild and unpredictable. Why? Sober upbringing, stable hard-working family, good marks at school. Everything perfect. And even if it had *not* been perfect I wouldn't have blamed them because here comes the sixth and most important thing I have to tell you: don't blame other people for what goes wrong in your own life. The only things you can blame are your genes. I *did* these awful things, I *watched* myself doing them, I *knew* they recurred again and again but I could do nothing about them and I never, never, never understood why. Somewhere inside me must be a gene that goes back God knows *where* to God knows *when* belonging to God knows *who* and *that's* a "why" you can't ever ask because a gene is a gene is a gene is a gene . . .'

> *Re-thinks that.*

Christ! What am I saying? That's depressing! Didn't I just now declare, only a minute ago: I refuse to be a prisoner of myself?

> *Wrestles with fears.*

The question is – the question is –

> *Her face lights up.*

The question is: has every gene in my body been activated?

> *Relieved, she sips her coffee.*

Thank God for espresso! (*Looking up.*) Thank you, God, for espresso!

> *She is boiling to say something that is obviously difficult for her, but by now she is high and determined.*

'Here, Marike, is my most difficult confession: I have never been in love. Can you believe it? Thirty-five years old, with a daughter of eleven, a "somebody" in the music business, my photo all over the place – I should have had the pick of men! Imagine me in the middle of the stage, my heart hanging out over the audience, my voice in full throttle, pushing back the air, the sweat of effort flowing from every pore, pouring from every crevice. Passion! A mesmerising energy drawing the attention of every man in the audience to every part of me, watching me, wearing their dreams around me, wanting me. And yet – I have never met a man *I* wanted. Isn't that strange? Don't you find that strange, daughter mine? There must be a reason.

What can it be?

'They say there are more interesting women in the world than men and – I don't know about the world – the *world*, I mean there's millions and millions in the *world* so we shouldn't generalise, but – in my experience, the women I meet, from all sorts of backgrounds, professions, countries, some have been married, some are single parents, some work hard at home, some at the top of their profession – nearly all of them tell me: they can't find a man! Not a really kind, gentle, tender, intelligent, imaginative, interesting, supportive thoughtful, respectful, educated, courageous, chivalrous, witty, thrilling, thrilling, thrilling man.

Dry irony –

'Perhaps we're asking too much!

Pause.

'Oh they can find a man to sleep with. It's never difficult to find a willing body. Your father was "a willing body". But a man to *love*?

She holds the word in the air.

'Love?

Pause.

'Make me feel? Really *feel*?

Long, long pause.

'Did I fear loss? Did I fear getting too close to someone I might lose? Close but not too close! Hold me but not too tight! Take your pleasure, give me some in exchange – then go! Poor men! My lips must have told them: your kisses don't claim me! They must have felt they were making love to the Ten Commandments! *Thou* shalt not, thou *shalt* not, thou shalt *not*!

Pause.

'Perhaps we should only expect three of those qualities.

Considers.

'But which three? Interesting, chivalrous, kind? Imaginative, witty, gentle? Thoughtful, thrilling, courageous?

'The trumpeter had none of those. (*To 'him'.*) Did you?

Enthusiastic. To daughter.

'*You* select, Marike. Look at my list and select which three qualities you would want in a man before you could love him. Add to my list and then choose. Do you want to be made to laugh, made to think, to be cared for, to care for? Do you want gentleness, firmness, predictability, *un*predictability? Make a long list then choose – three qualities.

Mood changes.

'And then forget them! For here's the seventh and most important thing I have to tell you: love has nothing to do with anything you dream or plan or decide for yourself. It may have more to do with smell, eyes, a smile, a setting, a trumpet! It makes no sense *when* it happens, *where* it happens, *how* it happens, or with *whom* it happens – which of course is a very good reason for avoiding it like the plague!

Bitter!

'I know what you're thinking. You're thinking – Mother, if you've never been in love how do you know these things? Well, the eighth and most important thing to tell you is: use your reason as much as possible but don't expect reason from human nature.'

Pause.

Why, *why* after eleven years?

She argues with herself.

Because the man has a daughter.

Not true! *I* have a daughter, he just tossed the seed over the fence.

Right! His seed. *His* seed.

Is seed all it takes to earn you a child?

To 'him'.

(*Mocking.*) 'Hi, Melanie. I know, I know you haven't heard from me in a long time . . .' A long time? Eleven fucking years long. And now, when I'm trying to pull my life together, building bridges with my daughter, you intrude, make me feel guilty of depriving her of a father she never had. I hate you. I've always hated you. In fact I hate all men.

Not true! Not true! Not true! Oh, God who art in heaven . . .

To Marike. Bitter, bitter!

'My dear daughter. This letter is going to be of no use to you at all.'

Desperate.

Damn and blast him! There must be something useful I can tell her after thirty-five years of a life.

Determined.

'My dear daughter. Here is the ninth and most important thing I have to tell you: men are the products of their mothers. Blame them for nothing. "Wrong" is its own gender – neither male nor female. Be a woman, but don't be smug! You like cooking? Cook! You like knitting? Knit! You want to be an astronaut? Be one! Study and take off! Me – I love cooking, hate knitting, am terrified of flying. Your tits are growing whether you like it or not; you're a woman whether you like it or not; your instincts will be feminine whether you like it or not. Neither good nor bad. Follow them, don't fight them. Just don't let anyone abuse you. And that's another action has its own gender – abuse.

She's on a roll now.

'I've known many women as well as men who got high on abusing others. Sweetness is not the prerogative of women. That's dogma. And here's the tenth and really most important thing I have to tell you: don't live by dogma – it's anti-human, bleak, sterile, the death of spontaneity, the death of creativity, the death of – oh – everything. No! You may need a father but not him. We can do better. Somewhere. Sooner or later. There! Resolved in one! No pussyfooting! Straight to the point – the way everything should be.'

Wait! Not so fast. Shouldn't I be giving her the choice?

No! I know her well enough to *know* she won't like him.

And no! I know her well enough to know she'll feel
guilty for not liking him. And no! I know her well
enough to know that from a misplaced sense of duty
she'll sacrifice herself and *pretend* she likes him. And
finally – I know she'll blame me for confronting her
with such an impossible *choice.*

On the other hand –

I also know that because parents never get it right she
would blame me if I *didn't* confront her with the choice.

Not true. She won't blame me. She'll thank me.

Not true. She'll blame me.

Not true. She'll thank me.

Blame me! Thank me! Thank me! Blame me! A gene!
A gene! My kingdom for the right gene.

> *Momentarily defeated until – a few lines from one of
> her songs floats into her consciousness. She sings:*

> . . . Said all the worthwhile loves
> Land in your hand with a tag-price
> Which you have to pay
> Sooner or later . . .

. . . sooner or later . . .

That's it! To 'him'.

Yes! *She* must decide, and loathe and despise you
though I do I'll pay that tag-price for my 'worthwhile
love' and I promise that if she asks, and only if *she* asks,
I'll tell her where you can be found and then – the
choice is hers.

Surprised.

Say! How about that? I didn't shoot first! Is it possible?

Maybe – maybe – your mother's found another gene. . . ?

Unties knot of her dressing-gown belt.

'My dear Marike. I wish I could *see* your future. Your *teacher* and *friends* tell me how special you are but when I kissed you good night in bed *I* could feel – your neck was stiff. Your great-*aunts* look at you and they say to me: "That one is in *tune* with herself! *There's* a girl full of harmony." But in the middle of the night *I* can hear – your teeth grind with anxiety . . .

'My dear daughter, Marike. I have been *meaning* to write to you for some time . . .'

'Audience' applause as lights fade.

Dressing-gown is off.

Something is about to happen.

She is on a stage – the Performer!

SONG SIX

It was our time

It was our time
Our time of youth
Festivity
Courage and delight
Will you remember?
Will you remember?
I will remember
It was our time of love
No heights we couldn't scale
No task we dared fail
Will you remember?
Will you remember?
I will remember
It was our time.

No one can take
From our time
No one can shake
The halcyon memories
When nothing was beyond
Our hopeful energies
And every day
In every way
It was our time.

It was our time
Balmy springtime
Serendipity
O I was pretty
So young and pretty
Remember?
Tender time

Reason and rhyme
Blessed never-ending time
Will you remember?
Will you remember?
I will remember
It was our time.

No one can take
From our time
No one can shake
The halcyon memories
When nothing was beyond
Our hopeful energies
No parents dead
No disappointments yet
No autumn
No black distress
No sadness yet
For what must pass
Remember?
Winter held no terror
When the spring returned
We would still be young
All would still be young
Will you remember?
Will you remember?
I will remember
It was our time.

No one can take
From our time
No one can shake
The halcyon memories
When nothing was beyond
Our hopeful energies
No parents dead
No disappointments yet

No autumn
No black distress
No sadness yet
And every day
In every way
It was our
It was our time
It was our time
It was our time.

Methuen Contemporary Dramatists
include

John Arden (two volumes)
Arden & D'Arcy
Peter Barnes (three volumes)
Sebastian Barry
Dermot Bolger
Edward Bond (six volumes)
Howard Brenton
  (two volumes)
Richard Cameron
Jim Cartwright
Caryl Churchill (two volumes)
Sarah Daniels (two volumes)
Nick Darke
David Edgar (three volumes)
Ben Elton
Dario Fo (two volumes)
Michael Frayn (three volumes)
David Greig
John Godber (two volumes)
Paul Godfrey
John Guare
Lee Hall (two volumes)
Peter Handke
Jonathan Harvey
  (two volumes)
Declan Hughes
Terry Johnson (two volumes)
Sarah Kane
Barrie Keefe
Bernard-Marie Koltès
David Lan
Bryony Lavery
Deborah Levy
Doug Lucie

David Mamet (four volumes)
Martin McDonagh
Duncan McLean
Anthony Minghella
  (two volumes)
Tom Murphy (four volumes)
Phyllis Nagy
Anthony Neilsen
Philip Osment
Louise Page
Stewart Parker (two volumes)
Joe Penhall
Stephen Poliakoff
  (three volumes)
David Rabe
Mark Ravenhill
Christina Reid
Philip Ridley
Willy Russell
Eric-Emmanuel Schmitt
Ntozake Shange
Sam Shepard (two volumes)
Shelagh Stephenson
Wole Soyinka (two volumes)
David Storey (three volumes)
Sue Townsend
Judy Upton
Michel Vinaver
  (two volumes)
Arnold Wesker (two volumes)
Michael Wilcox
Roy Williams
Snoo Wilson (two volumes)
David Wood (two volumes)
Victoria Wood

For a complete catalogue of Methuen Drama titles
write to:

Methuen Drama
11–12 Buckingham Gate
London SW1E 6LB

or you can visit our website at:

www.methuen.co.uk